CASE RECORDING IN SOCIAL WORK WITH CHILDREN AND FAMILIES

A straightforward and practical guide

By Rebecca O'Keefe and Siobhan Maclean

Kirwin Maclean
Associates

Published by Kirwin Maclean Associates

enquiries@kirwinmaclean.com
www.kirwinmaclean.com

First published in 2023
Kirwin Maclean Associates
4 Mesnes Green
Lichfield
Staffordshire
WS14 9AB
Graphic design by Tora Kelly
Printed and bound in Great Britain by 4edge, Essex

ISBN - 978-1-912130-51-1

eISBN - 978-1-912130-74-0

Cover design by Tora Kelly

Back cover illustration and illustration on page 68 by David Grimm

With thanks to the students and social workers who joined us to discuss their learning for the videos included in the book: Becky; Brett; Camilla; Cat; David; Elly; Jenna; Kai; Kelly; Kulchuma; Nicola; Noel and Sarah.

Contents

Foreword

A Note about the What? Why? How? Framework

The What? Why? How? framework (Maclean, 2019) is a simple and yet powerful framework for social work. A social worker starting work with a child should be able to answer the questions:

What is happening for this child?

Why has this situation come about?

How can I work with the child and their family to bring about change?

This basic structure can help aid reflection and decision making in social work practice. Research on social work supervision from Wilkins, Lynch and Antonopoulou (2018) demonstrates the importance of the What? Why? How? framework. The research team listened to audio recordings of supervision and, to decide whether they thought the supervision was practice-focused, they considered the questions:

1. Do we know what the social worker is going to do in the next home visit or the next few home visits with the family?
2. Do we understand why the social worker is going to do these things and how?
3. Has this discussion helped the social worker think more carefully about what they are going to do, and how and why?

In contemporary social work the why question seems to fall off the busy practitioner agenda. Social workers are much more likely to think 'what's happened? How do I respond?' With little focus on the why. There are many references to a loss of professional curiosity in social work practice, particularly in Serious Case Reviews (see chapter 9) and the dangers of this. Maintaining a balance with time spent on the why question is therefore important.

The What? Why? How? framework is especially helpful when thinking about social work record keeping. When reading a case file, the What? Why? and How? should be clear. For example:

What decision has been made?

Why has that decision been reached?

How has this decision been implemented and how is it impacting on the child and their family?

This is an important framework in social work, so this guide works through the What? Why? and How? of case recording in social work practice with children and families. The first three chapters, therefore, explore:

What is recording in social work?

Why is recording important?

Whilst the rest of the book takes a straightforward practical look at the question:

How should a social worker record?

The What? Why? How? framework is also used to encourage reflection at the end of each chapter.

Introduction

Case recording forms a significant part of a social worker's time. It is estimated that time spent on administrative tasks, which includes case recording, can be as high as 60-80% of a social worker's week (Holmes and McDermid, 2013). However, other studies have estimated that administration forms approximately a quarter of a social worker's time, and notwithstanding changes in technology, this is largely unchanged since the early 1970s (Baginsky et al., 2010). Writing is a key part of a social worker's day, nestled between other activities, with time spent on writing largely underestimated by staff (Lillis et al., 2020).

The 'Independent Review of Children's Social Care' in England (2022) recognises that action for *"improving case management systems, reducing repetitive administrative tasks which do not add value"* is very much needed in social work with children and families (MacAllister, 2022: 11). We agree and welcome this acknowledgement for social work and social care staff. However, despite a lack of consensus regarding exactly how much time is actually spent on case recording and other office-based tasks, it is unquestionably an inevitable and necessary part of the job and will continue to be so. Eileen Munro, in her review of child protection (2011: 111), states *"recording is a key social work task and its centrality in the protection of children cannot be over-estimated"*. Learning skills in how to record information concisely, efficiently and creatively will not only help you manage your own time but also promote critical thinking and reflection in your everyday work.

This guide will explore what high-quality case recording looks like. It will give helpful written examples, questions to reflect upon in your own daily practice, and creative ideas to use. The guide covers case recording in work with children and families, although many of the fundamental principles covered also relate to social work with adults.

As you read this book, you will realise the importance and power of our language and the words we use. The phrase 'case recording' in the title, for us, refers to the process of capturing events in a child or young person's life and documenting the important work we do with families. We consciously recognise the word 'case' in this context is very much a professional term and one which children and families could misinterpret. In her excellent blog entitled 'Rewriting social care', Bryony Shannon (2019) highlights the word 'case' when used outside of a professional context means 'baggage'. The word therefore has very different connotations. She emphasises social workers sometimes talk about 'cases', 'caseloads' and 'case management' with individuals becoming 'passive recipients', rather than individuals or people. This can dehumanise those we work with, and children and young people can become lost. Although we do use the word 'case' in this guide as it is used and understood within the social work profession, we strongly advocate for children, young people and their families being recognised and described as individuals within their written records, and speaking of children, young people and families, rather than 'cases', in our verbal discussions.

In Chapter 1, we will consider what is included under the umbrella term 'case recording' and what written documents you may see or be asked to complete as a social worker. Chapter 2 reflects upon why case recording is so important for children, young people and their families, as well as for other stakeholders, such as multi-agency professionals and organisations. We encourage you to consider how case recording is integral to forming relationships with children, young people and families and how it can really enhance the work we do. The basics of case recording is the focus of Chapter 3. We cover what is important to capture in case recording, with ideas for how we can do this well in practice. Chapter 4 is a compilation of writing from care experienced social workers who have accessed their own files, their reflections add a powerful dimension to this book. Chapter 5 concentrates on social work visits, recognising the complexity of obtaining and capturing information when we step into the homes of children, young people and families. An area which is not always considered in detail is how we record social work meetings. Chapter 6 looks at this area specifically, reflecting on how the planning and facilitation of meetings can also significantly influence case recording. We share views of care experienced people and their advocates in Chapter 7, emphasising the additional responsibilities we have in terms of case recording for children and young people who are or have been care experienced. Chapter 8 covers analysis in case recording providing a range of practical tools. Chapter 9 shares lessons learned from Child Safeguarding Practice Reviews and Serious Case Reviews over the years in relation to case recording, including the very recent tragic deaths of Arthur Labinjo-Hughes and Star Hobson, which prompted a national review. Finally, we draw our knowledge together to offer practical tips for good quality case recording in Chapter 10.

The What? Why? How? framework is used to encourage reflection at the end of each chapter. We hope you will pause and consider how your learning can be embedded in social work practice and we offer opportunity for you to connect with knowledge and enhance your own case recording skills. You will find points in the guide to 'focus on practice' and 'pause for reflection'. These sections can be considered on your own, with peers and co-workers, or perhaps within whole teams as reflective exercises. These sections of the guide allow you to reflect deeper on the content you have read, as well as on the case recording you have done or have seen in real life social work practice, further championing good practice in case recording in the important work you do every day.

In working together to develop this guide, we wanted to provide more than a simple 'book'. We have, therefore, met to discuss each chapter, sometimes with social workers and others, and we have recorded these discussions. A QR code at the end of each chapter will take you to the video. We hope that this may add another dimension to the guide and be particularly useful for visual learners.

To try out this interactive feature in the text you may want to start by watching this webinar on recording in social work.

This is a webinar hosted by the Social Work Student Connect Team. A number of experienced social workers join the team to share their experiences of recording and report writing. A range of practical tips are included.

Chapter 1

What is Case Recording in Social Work?

Dictionary definitions demonstrate that recording is essentially about capturing what has happened. For example, recording a sound or a performance for subsequent reproduction or broadcast. In social work recording, we are capturing what is happening for a child or young person and what involvement we may have in their lives. Everything that a social worker does with an individual must be recorded and this recording is brought together to form a case file. The case file refers to the collation of all the information in one place, whether this be in paper format, electronically, or a combination of both.

Case recording is not simply a daily record or diary. It is powerful tool to reflect upon, and to aid analysis and planning. Good case notes form the foundation for other essential documents within the case file, such as assessments, reports, chronologies, and care plans. Ray Jones advises viewing social work case recording in four distinct parts, namely:

- The running record of information and action
- Regular summaries
- Assessment and reviews
- Plans

(Jones, 2016: 33)

The running record forms the foundation of all other parts of the case file. Summaries will be determined by the amount of activity which takes place, and the rate and pace of change. Assessments, reviews and plans are updated at regular intervals, or when significant changes have occurred.

What kind of records do we keep in social work?

There are a number of components to a case file, which may vary from organisation to organisation. There is also some diversity in terms of whether the file relates to a child or an adult, or sometimes the whole family. The following documents are common within many children's social work case files:

- Referrals
- Case notes
- Genogram
- Ecomap
- Chronology
- Assessments
- Plans
- Correspondence
- Risk alerts
- Decision making tools
- Decisions
- Summaries
- Specific forms

As you can see, there are many components to a child's file and many different documents you may be expected to record on. When you are new, it is important to familiarise yourself with your agency's own system and talk to experienced social workers about what is recorded in a child's file, where and how. This will be different across different organisations. You could use this list of common documents in conversation with colleagues or your manager, if you are starting a new role or are beginning a new social work placement, for example. Documents will differ between organisations and may look different on a computerised system or be called different names to those in our list.

Using the What? Why? and How? framework this chapter works through each of these records, considering what it is and why we do it. Some aspects of how we should complete the record is included in this chapter, although subsequent chapters go into more detail in relation to particular records.

Referrals

Effectively there are two types of referrals to consider in recording: referrals into your service and referrals going out of your service.

Referrals in

Due to the high demand upon social work front door services, many organisations have now introduced a distinction between 'referral' and 'contact'. Social workers need to be aware of what these terms mean, not only to inform their own practice, but to be able to communicate the difference to multi-agency colleagues and the public.

A 'contact' is the incoming information from an outside agency or member of the public, which is logged as information only. This requires no further action by the social work service but may involve some liaison with or signposting to an alternative service, such as a community organisation, education or health professional.

A 'referral' is incoming information which leads to a response by the social work service. Both a contact and a referral will include the date the information was obtained, by whom and what information was provided on this date. It will say who received the information; their designation within your service; and what decision was made at this point and why.

The Government's guidance entitled 'Working Together to Safeguard Children: Statutory guidance on inter-agency working to safeguard and promote the welfare of children' (HM Government, 2018), often referred to as Working Together 2018, is clear that once a referral is accepted by a local authority social work service, a social worker should acknowledge receipt of the information with the referrer within one working day and make a decision regarding next steps. The social worker becomes the lead professional. Next steps can be:

- *"the child requires immediate protection and urgent action is required*
- *the child is in need and should be assessed under section 17 of the Children Act 1989*

- *there is reasonable cause to suspect that the child is suffering or likely to suffer significant harm, and whether enquires must be made and the child assessed under section 47 of the Children Act 1989*
- *services are required by the child and family and what type of services*
- *further specialist assessments are required to help the local authority to decide what further action to take*
- *to see the child as soon as possible if the decision is taken that the referral requires further assessment."*

(HM Government, 2018: 30)

For referrers, the process can sometimes be confusing, and this has been highlighted as an area for multi-agency learning from Child Safeguarding Practice Reviews (CSPR's), previously known as Serious Case Reviews (SCRs). Often this is due to professionals not fully understanding the child protection process, or being inexperienced in referring information (SCIE, 2016). Difficulties have arisen when the referrer was not made aware that their information was classified as a contact only, and they believed a referral had been made.

If you are asked to work with a child or family where there has been no previous involvement with the service, you may only have the referral to read. If there has been previous service involvement you may see multiple previous referrals and contacts recorded. You should be able to see a clear link from the historical referrals to any assessments previously completed and what interventions were undertaken.

Referrals out

When you are working with a child or young person you may feel that they, or their family, would benefit from support from another organisation. In this case, you will need to complete a referral to that organisation. Every organisation will receive referrals in different ways, and you may need to complete a specific document. When completing a referral, it is always good practice to do so alongside the child and family concerned – what do they want you to include? How would they describe the support they need?

Case notes

A case note is the recorded detail of one specific interaction, such as a phone call, visit or meeting. Everything must be recorded. If a phone call was made but there was no answer, this should be recorded. Case notes become the daily log of what is happening. Case notes will inevitably vary in length and level of detail and require professional judgement on what information is to be included. For phone calls, for example, it is important to always include the name, profession (where appropriate) or relationship to the child of the person with whom you have communicated, as well as their contact details, such as up to date phone numbers.

Usually, a case note will document factual information followed by professional judgement. So, what has been said, heard or observed, and based on this information, what it means for the individual. Case notes should make explicit what information is factual and what information is the professional judgement of the writer. It's important to record accurate views and opinions of the individuals you've engaged with whether these be the child or young person themselves, their wider family members or professionals. Any direct quotes should be in quotation marks.

Electronic communication, such as email or SMS (Short Message Service), including text messages, can be considered efficient and more accessible forms of communication, often favoured by some young people, parents and carers, thus becoming everyday forms of communication for social workers. Emails can be directly cut and pasted into a case note or downloaded and attached as a document; text messages can be directly copied or perhaps screenshot with the photograph uploaded onto the social work system. Knowledge of your own electronic recording system and practice within your organisation is vital here, as these forms of communication can be a little tricky to record and you need to be doing this consistently with peers and colleagues.

Be mindful of professionalism when writing emails and text messages as, by their very nature, they are designed to be less formal and more brief, than letters for example. Remember, all forms of communication should reflect our *"professional purpose, legal obligations and ethical standards"* to reinforce the professional nature of the relationship (Healy and Mulholland, 2019: 64). When emails and text messages are recorded on a child's case file, ensure they make sense to the reader. Be wary of 'email trails' where lots of people reply to an email, and there is a long chain of responses. This can problematic if cut and pasted directly into a case note, as an email trail can be difficult to interpret and be very lengthy. Text messages, or other SMS communication is useful and sometimes more accessible for young people and adults, but again it can be difficult to record. Although more concise, professional text messages should be written using conventional grammar and punctuation (Healy and Mulholland, 2019). You may need to add information if a response, such as from a young person, isn't clear to the reader.

Pause for Reflection

It would be useful to consider good practice when recording individual case notes, especially emails and text messages, which often spark debate within social work practice. Using the What? Why? How? framework, consider the following reflective questions:

What do you consider to be important in recording case notes?

Why is recording case notes so important?

How will you use knowledge from this section to record individual case notes, especially email and text messages, in future?

We will consider these questions in more detail in later chapters.

Genograms

Genograms are a pictorial representation of the relationships someone has within their family, providing a visual picture of the individual's biological network. Genograms are important to identify family relationships and how they link to the individual. They are an excellent way to clarify complex relationships and can illustrate intergenerational patterns and gaps in professional knowledge about the family.

In a genogram, specific symbols are used to represent family members, and lines connect them. For example, a circle depicts females and squares depict males, with a triangle illustrating pregnancy, miscarriage, or abortion. Names and ages are written within the shapes. Solid horizontal lines represent marriage, and horizontal vertical lines represent parentage. A dotted line denotes non-married relationships. There are a wide range of symbols and lines which can represent the most complex of families. Being able to create and to understand a comprehensive genogram is an important skill to learn. It is always helpful to print out the genogram and check details with the family directly. This also allows transparency between the professional and the family regarding what information is recorded about them, and how this is stored.

Some computer systems, used for case recording by social workers, can generate genograms for you. However, you must ensure the details of each family member and their relationship to the child are entered correctly to ensure its accuracy, and you should always check what is generated.

Genograms are not only useful for gathering information, but they can also be used creatively to work directly with children and their families, by exploring family dynamics in more depth (Race and O'Keefe, 2017). This can help families examine their relationships, and understand behaviours, patterns and functioning. Genograms can be creative, visual and fun, especially when completed in direct work with children. A small toy or object could be chosen to represent family members, or coloured pens and simple drawings could be used to explore a child's understanding of their family relationships. To inform an assessment, or as part of understanding their family history, a more informal 'family tree' could be completed with a child or young person. Grandparents and 'ancestors' could be the roots, parents or carers, the branches, and children depicted as the leaves (Race and O'Keefe, 2017: 154). A photograph of the final piece should be taken and uploaded to the child's electronic file. The child could keep their completed piece and this can be referred back to as needed.

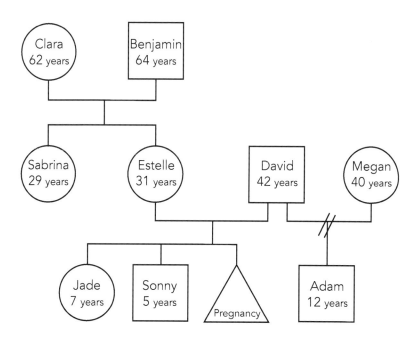

Genogram explanation

This very simple genogram shows various family members with a square representing a male and circle a female. Estelle and David are in a relationship with two children, Jade and Sonny, and the triangle represents a pregnancy, so they also have a baby on the way. The two marks on the line between David and Megan represent a divorce. Megan and David also have one son together called Adam. Estelle's parents, Benjamin and Clara, and her sister, Sabrina, are present on the genogram. However, we have no further information for David and Megan.

Ecomaps

Whilst genograms are about family and biological networks, an ecomap highlights connections between an individual and their "*ecological environment*" (Maclean and Harrison, 2015: 198).

Ecomaps are sometimes referred to as sociograms. They were developed as a social work tool by Ann Hartman in the 1970s. The idea of the ecomap is to highlight all of the connections that an individual has. Identifying the connections should include highlighting the strength of connections and can also demonstrate energy flowing in and out of an individual and possibly their family, so that the reciprocity of relationships and access to resources / networks become clear (Hartman, 1995).

In relation to evidencing wider support networks for an individual, such as family friends, professionals, peers, neighbours, community resources and professional relationships, an ecomap may be appropriate. An ecomap gives a detailed picture of family dynamics; the family's connection to the community; their support system; areas of deprivation where resources may be provided; or service duplication (Social Work Toolbox, 2019).

In developing an ecomap, it is vital to ask the child and their family who is important to them, without asking leading questions or making assumptions. It will give you a really useful insight into how the child views their support network.

Ecomap styles vary but generally they consist of circles and lines. A solid line generally indicates a strong and healthy relationship, a zig zag line often indicates a relationship involving conflict or stress, a broken line generally indicates a weaker relationship. Often arrows are added to demonstrate the flow of energy between relationships. Broken relationships may be represented by a cross over the line. Because styles differ, a key must always be provided with the ecomap.

Exploring the family's network can help to identify strengths to build upon. For example, if there is a positive relationship with a child's school, an educational professional may take the lead with parenting work or direct work with the child. If a family friend is very supportive, they may be able to provide practical or emotional support in a regular and planned way, and be a formal part of the individual's plan. The ecomap may also form the basis for the individuals who could attend a family group conference, for example.

Using an ecomap creatively with a child or young person can be really useful. Beginning with the child's name in the centre of a large piece of paper, with the child having control over who and what is important to them represented on the page. They could include family and friends, pets, hobbies and interests, and key professionals. Drawings or small objects, such as toys or buttons of difference shapes, colours or sizes, could represent people and places. However, it is important that *"adult interpretations are not placed on children's ideas in the process"*; for example, a child may choose a spider to represent their father, *"not because he is scary, but because they love spiders"* (Race and O'Keefe, 2017: 154). Listening to and engaging with the child or young person is key in the process, and a creative ecomap can be really helpful to form a clearer understanding of the child's world.

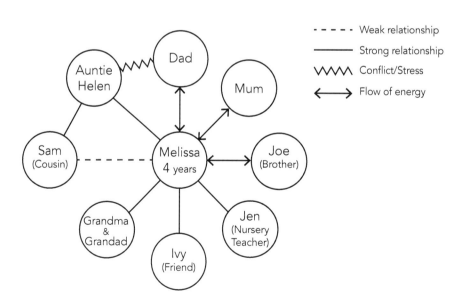

Ecomap explanation

This very simple ecomap is for Melissa (4 years). As we can see she appears to have a strong relationship with her mother, father and brother with a flow of energy to and from these relationships. We can see a conflictual or stressful relationship between Melissa's father and her aunt Helen, and a weak relationship between Melissa and her cousin, Sam. She has other strong relationships with her friend, Ivy, Jen (the nursery teacher), and her grandparents.

If you use a genogram or ecomap to gather initial information, to complete direct work, or as part of an assessment, you should scan and upload the document to your computer system. The child or their family may wish to keep a copy of their genogram or ecomap. This is especially important if the piece of work has helped them make connections in their own family, evoked strong emotions, or allowed them to reflect on their life experiences and community support. You can refer to the genogram and ecomap at a later point to look at any changes in family dynamics or extended support or add information. It should be a living document rather than a completed form.

It is important to involve children and their families in the development of ecomaps and genograms. Ecomaps, in particular, are ideal to do with children. You can use buttons, toys or anything else to represent different people. Ask the child why they have chosen a particular button or toy to represent the person, and this will help you to understand more about how they see their relationships.

So, in summary, remember genograms are factual documents: what are this individual's family / biological networks? Ecomaps are more evaluative: how does this person see their relationships?

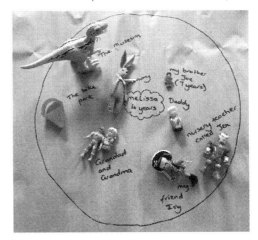

Chronology

A chronology is simply a record of events or dates in the order of their occurrence. Chronologies can be very helpful in all areas of social work to understand what has happened in someone's life and to learn about service involvement. However, they are most commonly used in social work with children and families.

In social work with children a chronology is an essential element of the social work file. Every child should have an up to date chronology recorded on their case file. This is the primary source of information to read when accessing a case file for the first time, as it gives an overview of the child's life and service involvement to date. In the event there is a need for pre-proceedings or Court intervention, the chronology is one of the first documents you will be asked to present (Ministry of Justice, 2021).

Put simply, the chronology is the significant events or changes in a child or young person's life recorded in date order. They are logical and systematic, merging and making sense of information (Calder, 2016). There should be no professional judgements recorded. For most chronologies, the following events are relevant: *"births; deaths; marriages; house moves; serious illness; changes in household composition; changes in legal status; arrests and court appearances; educational achievement; employment status; child protection case conferences"* (Care Inspectorate, 2017: 11). The chronology starts from the child's birth, or sometimes earlier if there is social work intervention during pregnancy, rather than from the initial involvement with your service.

Although the chronology is not an assessment, it does require professional knowledge and skill. The chronology is vital to informing any assessment. As Dyke asserts:

"So why, in many teams, are chronologies treated as an administrative task, a tiresome bureaucratic exercise to be done as an afterthought? Why are so many teams prepared to delegate chronologies to unqualified staff who would never be expected to write the assessment? Why do so many workers say "I've done the

assessment, now I've got to do the chronology" when the one is impossible without the other."

(Dyke, 2019: 19)

Ofsted's national director for social care, Yvette Stanley, wrote a blog on case recording, highlighting the significance of a thorough chronology, stating *"an excellent chronology becomes like a map that navigates you through a child's life. It can be incredibly frustrating when its order does not make sense"* (Stanley, 2019).

Missing information in chronologies, or no chronology recorded at all, is often highlighted as a contributory factor in poor decision making, leading to failure to sufficiently safeguard children. High profile child deaths over the last four decades, from Maria Colwell to Victoria Climbie and beyond, have highlighted a systematic chronology could have assisted in preventing tragedy (Laming, 2003; Pemberton, 2010). The independent inquiry led by Alexis Jay into child sexual exploitation in Rotherham stated:

"There was a chronology in fewer than half the cases (43%) where it would have been appropriate to have one – and most chronologies were out of date, with significant gaps. It is likely that the absence of structured chronologies contributed to key information being missed when decisions were made."

(Jay, 2014: 48)

It is important that social workers recognise how risks and needs might change over time, taking account of this in their practice and *"relevant professionals can only fully achieve this if they identify and understand the significant patterns and trends in circumstances that an effectively prepared chronology will reveal"* (Care Inspectorate 2017: 4).

When embarking on a chronology, think of it as a stand-alone document. Someone unfamiliar with the case should be able to read only the chronology and gain a good understanding of the child's life: what has happened to them and their family, and when it happened. There should be sufficient detail, but not so much detail that it is merely a repeat of daily case recording. Some computer systems have the option to pull through a case note directly into the chronology at the push of a button, with the intention to save social workers' time. However, often the amount of information within the case note is unnecessary for the chronology and makes it too lengthy and detailed. Remember if you do pull through case notes, always go to the chronology to check and amend the information, to make it clear and concise.

The chronology does require professional judgement, and consideration of what information is relevant to build a comprehensive picture. A child missing from school may not appear to be a significant event in its own right, but in the context of Child Sexual Exploitation (CSE) or child neglect for example, documenting periods of school absence may be highly significant. Documenting every aspect of a child's health information, such as accessing the GP, hospital or NHS walk-in centre, may not be relevant for the majority of chronologies, but may be necessary for a child where the concern is possibly fabricated or induced illness or non-accidental injuries.

There has been criticism of poor-quality chronologies, especially in cases of neglect. The focus has been on 'key events in the life of the family rather than a cumulative record of ongoing neglect and its impact on the child' (Ofsted, 2014: 19). This emphasises the skill required not only in undertaking a comprehensive chronology but interpreting the information and fully understanding the impact on the child to inform decision making. Collaboration with other agencies may be required in very complex cases, with an interagency chronology undertaken (Calder, 2015).

Excerpt of a chronology for a young child

Date	Event
28th November 2022	Police attend the family home. A neighbour reported hearing shouting and screaming at the property. On arrival of the Police, Aisha has a black eye. She shared she is pregnant. Her husband, Nadhim, had already left the property. Aisha attends hospital with the Police, so that she can be checked, but discharges herself before being seen.
29th November 2022	A referral to the Children's Social Work Service is received from the Police with concerns for unborn Khan. The Police refer to the incident on the 28th November but also have two verbal disputes recorded, both in August 2021, at the property.

2nd December 2022	Aisha is contacted by Kim Holland (social worker) by telephone. She states 'everything is now ok' and she does not want to see a social worker as it will 'make things worse'. She puts down the phone. Further calls do not connect.
4th December 2022	Unannounced visit completed to the family home at 10.45am. No response. However, the curtains appear to move in the upstairs bedroom.
5th December 2022	Unannounced social work visit at 4.30pm. Aisha answers the door, but does not allow Kim Holland (social worker) in. She says Nadhim will be home from work soon and will be angry if sees a social worker. A visit is arranged at the office for the next day.
6th December 2022	Aisha does not attend the social work office as arranged. A phone call is made to Aisha, but the phone does not connect.
8th December 2022	Aisha attends the social work office alone at 9am. She states she is scared of her husband but cannot leave him. She is worried for her baby who is due on 24th January 2022. Aisha has been having pains in her abdomen for two days and agrees to attend hospital. The social worker takes her to the maternity ward. Aisha has a scan, all is fine and she is discharged.
15th December 2022	Kiran is born at 5.52am at St Gemma's University Hospital. She is 36 weeks gestation. Kiran is the daughter of Aisha and Nadhim. Nadhim is present at the birth.
16th December 2022	The staff nurse contacts the Children's Social Work Service and shares some concerns. Nadhim was seen to become angry with Aisha when she was trying to feed Kiran. The nurse challenged Nadhim and he said sorry and he was very tired. He went off the ward for a cigarette.
18th December 2022	Phone call by social worker to the ward to arrange hospital visit. Aisha and Kiran remain in hospital as Kiran is struggling to feed. Aisha appears very tearful and low in mood. Nadhim is described as 'attentive towards Kiran'. Nadhim has shared with staff he has recently lost his job and the couple are struggling financially.

Assessments

Assessment work is acknowledged as a core task in social work practice. Good assessments can contribute to better outcomes. For example, a comprehensive assessment can improve the chances of reunification for children and young people and influence the effective targeting of interventions (Turney et al., 2011). Assessments may also identify needs, strengths, risks, best interests or capacity. Assessment is increasingly acknowledged as the continuous process of planning, intervening and reviewing (Parker, 2017).

There are numerous excellent texts on conducting social work assessments, which will give helpful advice and information on this aspect of case recording. Fundamentally, the purpose of an assessment is always about gathering and analysing information to reach a decision which can be used to inform future outcomes. Working Together 2018 makes clear the purpose of assessment within children and families is always:

- *"to gather important information about a child and family*
- *to analyse their needs and / or the nature and level of any risk and harm being suffered by the child*
- *to decide whether the child is a child in need (section 17) or is suffering or likely to suffer significant harm (section 47)*
- *to provide support to address those needs to improve the child's outcomes and welfare and where necessary to make them safe."*

(HM Government, 2018: 23)

In practice, assessments can look and feel very different. Local authorities will have their own templates for assessments. In children and families practice, these will be based on the assessment framework, often referred to as the 'assessment triangle' (HM Government, 2018: 30). This provides an overarching conceptual framework, rather than an instruction manual for social work assessments (Turney et al., 2011), based on three domains: the child's developmental needs; parenting capacity; and family and environmental factors (HM Government, 2018). Assessments will always include the wishes and feelings of the child; speaking with the child's parents or carers; and acquiring information from all professionals who have knowledge of the family to ensure a holistic overview.

Some assessments will be short pieces of work to determine if there is a current risk to a child; if there is a need for social work intervention; or what immediate support is required. A longer, more in-depth assessment may be required, where there are multiple issues, or due to the complexity or seriousness of a case. All assessments should include analysis of the information obtained and make clear recommendations. The maximum timescale for completing an assessment for a child and their family is 45 working days (HM Government, 2018). A timescale will be agreed with your team manager, as the whole 45 days may not be necessary, and this avoids delay for the family.

There may be a need for social workers to carry out specialist assessments. These are usually led by more experienced social workers, or those who have completed additional, specialist training. For example, a specialist deafblind assessment will be carried out by someone with specific knowledge and training. An assessment in pregnancy or involving a parent with a learning disability will require specialist skills. There may be specific proformas or frameworks within your agency to undertake more complex pieces of assessments.

If a case remains open on a longer-term basis, your organisation will have guidance on how often an assessment needs to be formally updated. This is usually at least annually, or when significant changes have occurred.

Plans

Where there is ongoing work with an individual there will always be a plan. This might be referred to as a care plan, intervention plan or support plan - but essentially it is about the work that is being undertaken with a child, young person or family.

All children with social work involvement will have a care plan, which is inherently linked to the outcome of any completed assessment work. There may be a range of plans depending on the nature of the child's situation, ranging from child in need to child protection. If a child becomes looked after by the local authority, the child will have a Child Looked After (CLA) plan. There will be a range of reports and written plans required depending on the nature of the family situation, and these include:

- Child in need plan
- Education, health and care plan for a child with a disability
- Child protection plan
- Child Looked After (CLA) plan
- Personal Education Plan (PEP) for a child looked after
- Pathway plan for a child leaving the care of the local authority.

Your organisation will have clear procedures in relation to each of these plans, with specific timescales for completion and sharing information with the child and their family. It is essential you familiarise yourself with your local procedures.

Correspondence

Any written information to or from outside agencies, the individual or their family, such as letters or reports, will be recorded in a correspondence section of a case file, again in paper format or electronically. This could be appointment letters or information sent to the child or their family by the social worker; health or educational reports; letters from the child or their family; court documents; or other information from outside agencies. Any sent and received information recorded in the correspondence section should be highlighted in case notes, with an obvious link on how to access the primary document. If relevant, significant information received should also be recorded in the chronology.

Risk Alerts

A social work file will highlight any personal risks to be aware of when working with an individual or family. It could be to highlight a vicious dog at the property; a family member who has a violent history or specific conviction; someone who has made threats to a professional; or to ensure visits are always completed with a colleague and not alone. Risk alerts can be inputted by the social worker, in discussion with the team manager, to ensure the safety of any colleague in the department who may come into contact with an individual or family. This information needs to be reviewed regularly to ensure it is not only up to date, but to ensure accuracy and fairness to the family. Risk alerts can mean that people pre-judge a situation, so whilst it is important to read a file to take account of risks, it is vital to be aware of how this could create a bias or pre-conception.

 Decisions

Decision making is intellectually and emotionally challenging. Making proactive and reflective decisions based on sound case recording is vital to meaningful, positive work. Decision making is therefore fundamentally linked to good case recording overall.

Social workers in child protection can be reluctant to make proactive decisions, often procrastinating, with decisions often being made in crisis (Munro, 2002). This can result in poor planning and drift for vulnerable children and their families. In relation to recording on the child's file, formal decisions are documented separately and should be easy to access and understand. These will be primarily management decisions, informed by discussion with the child's social worker, reports and assessments completed, and the information recorded on the child's file. Decisions should be evidence informed and should explicitly refer to local procedures, and national policy and legislation, where relevant. When reading the child's file, it should be clear when and why a decision has been made, and by whom.

There are a wide range of important decisions which should be recorded including, but not exclusively:

- Action required following referral
- The outcome of an assessment and plan of action
- The outcome of specific enquiries (for example, a section 47 enquiry)
- Action required following a significant event
- Reason for case transfer or case closure
- Reason for change of social worker
- Legal advice and legal action
- The outcome of local panels, such as risk management panels, fostering panels, or higher management decisions.

There are occasions when you may not wholly agree with a management decision for a child or family you are working with, and this can be very challenging for the social worker. It is important that issues are openly discussed with your team manager, or higher managers, and explored objectively based on the information available. Direct conversations are more useful than email exchanges, for example. However, if differences of opinion are recorded, they should always be done so in a respectful and professional manner.

Decision making tools

Over the last few years, a number of tools have been developed to support social workers (and other professionals) to reach clear decisions. If a tool has been used in decision making, this will need to be explicit within the case file, maybe with the tool used saved onto the child's file if required. Tools may include:

- a process map which considers whether all the stages of a process have been followed
- a checklist based on an understanding of risk indicators
- a screening tool based on facts in a situation.

Decision making tools are often based on research or facts but will also include some analysis – for example, weighing up the costs and benefits of a decision. Brown et al. (2017) identified that there were between nine and 28 different assessment tools and checklists used in relation to child sexual exploitation across England and Wales. These were wide-ranging: "*in particular, we found that the risk indicators being used varied considerably across the large number of tools in operation. An examination of 10 tools identified 110 different indicators, with each tool having a different combination of these.*" (Brown et al., 2017: 9). The number of tools available for social workers can be overwhelming. It is important to be clear about what the tool was designed for, why you are using it and how it will influence your decision.

 ## Summaries

A social work case summary reviews the work completed and any events and changes over time in a succinct and clear way. Getting into a habit of completing regular summaries will improve your analytical skills and ensure critical thinking throughout your work. It will also assist in minimising drift. There may be specific guidance in your organisational procedures for how frequently case summaries are expected, and what to include. You should always follow these procedures in the first instance. However, a summary at least every three months, whilst the case remains open, is a good rule of thumb. You will need to use your professional judgement whether a summary would be helpful more frequently, for example, if you have a complicated case, or a significant event occurs which changes the plan of action.

As a busy practitioner, summaries can sometimes feel like a duplication of your case notes, appear time consuming and perhaps unnecessary. However, if completed regularly they are an excellent tool for reflection. Summaries will ultimately save you time, as your work will be thoughtful, focused and proactive. They give you an opportunity to review the work which has taken place in a specific period, and a chance to reflect on your own case recordings. They help formulate a plan of action or 'what next?' for a child and family.

Summaries are especially useful for managers and colleagues who need to access your work quickly if you are unavailable. If you are going on planned leave then it is important that you complete a brief summary for each child wherever possible, so that others will know what has been happening, should they need to become involved in your absence. It needs to be clear what is happening currently in the child's life, and what the up-to-date plan is.

Summaries can be used as a practical tool. Taking a recently completed case summary to supervision with your line manager will help you both to focus on next steps, consider what additional support may be required, and inform your decision making. Sharing a case summary openly with an individual or their family will allow reflection on their progress and achievements, as well as exploring difficulties and challenges. Sharing information allows transparency and the opportunity for individuals to give their direct views. These views should be formally recorded.

Focus on Practice

Before completing a summary, you could ask yourself the following reflective 'what?' questions:

What significant events or changes have occurred since the last summary was completed?

What are the objectives of the child's plan? Are they being met?

What strengths can you identify?

What needs to happen to make further progress?

You could also ask the child or adult and their family these questions directly. This will help openly explore the barriers to a plan progressing, or highlight achievements, and you can share your views with them. Regular feedback will help keep the plan on track and provide support and encouragement. Can the child or family complete their own summary or contribute to the summary to enhance collaboration?

A transfer summary will be required if a case is to move to another team within your organisation, such as a Child Looked After (CLA) team, or to another local authority if the child moves area. A closure summary is completed when all work has come to an end, as a conclusion to the work completed. Transfer and closure summaries may be longer than regular case summaries, as they need to be a complete summary of the entirety of the intervention. Again, it is likely your organisation will have a case transfer and / or closure summary template or proforma, but the following information is always useful to include:

- Basic details such as full name, dates of birth and addresses
- Brief history if the child or family is previously known to your service
- Reason for the most recent episode of social work involvement, including referral information
- The child or young person's views (and family member or carers as relevant)
- Summary of assessment work, including outcomes and recommendations
- Type of plan implemented, and what specific work was completed as part of the plan (key professional details are always useful to include with contact details)
- Significant events which have occurred during the social work involvement, including dates and any action undertaken
- Strengths
- Recommendation of further work required, if any.

 Specific forms

There will be a wide range of forms which make up case recording which we have not explored in this chapter. The format used may vary in terms of context and time – so different agencies require the completion of different forms. Forms can feel very repetitive when you consider what else you are recording in relation a child's life and your involvement with them. However, if they are required it is important to complete the forms well. Forms may be used for specific audit purposes or to review what is happening in a particular geographical area, thereby informing service provision or the allocation of resources.

Electronic recording systems

As stated, many social work organisations now have electronic systems which will 'pull through' specific information for particular forms. It is vital though that social workers recognise professional responsibility extends to ensuring that the information which is pulled through is accurate, and that the form is completed to a good professional standard. Electronic systems should aid the social workers rather than directing or replacing the social worker. In some areas electronic algorithms are starting to be used to consider risk. Again, these should not direct decision making but rather they should be seen as offering support in decision making. Social workers need to employ critical analysis in their use of all recording tools.

Conclusion

This chapter has considered all the elements which are likely to be present in the case files for children and families with whom you are working. We have considered good practice, professional expectations and creative methods to engage with families in a more collaborative way, using elements of the child's case file as practical tools to increase analysis and critical thinking. As a final reflection using the What? Why? How? framework:

What have you learned from this chapter that will be useful for your own case recording?

Why is this learning important?

How will this knowledge influence your own case recording?

 Talking it Through

It is always important to extend your learning and talking things through with others can be helpful. At the end of each chapter we include a link to a video showing some students and / or practitioners talking through the content and their learning. In this video Siobhan and Rebecca meet with Brett, a social work student, Kulchuma a newly qualified school based social worker and Becky a social worker who works with children with disabilities. They share their learning from reading this chapter.

Chapter

2

Why is Recording Important in Social Work with Children and Families?

One of the most important questions we can ask in any situation is 'why?' The leadership consultant Simon Sinek created the 'golden circle' asserting that effective leadership and learning starts with why. Sinek claims that *"if you don't know why, you can't know how"* (Sinek 2019: 70). Sinek's most well-known book is called 'Start with Why'. Good social work always starts with why? 'Why am I working with this child? Why am I involved in this family's life?' Clarity of involvement is key to the work that we do, and hypotheses are developed from an initial starting point of asking why?

Thinking through a range of answers to the question 'why is this happening?' can aid analysis and decision making, and is a key aspect of professional curiosity, which is vital in social work practice and yet has been found lacking in a number of high-profile cases. Understanding why something needs to happen has been widely evidenced to improve motivation and, therefore, starting with why can also assist with using motivational techniques with children and their families. Sinek, Mead and Docker (2017) assert that being clear about why we are doing things improves confidence and job satisfaction which could offer a great deal to social workers in the current climate of practice. Since 'why?' is such an important question, this short chapter will consider exactly why recording is so important. Understanding the fundamental basis for record keeping will help you consider and review your own recording practice. Pritchard and Leslie (2011) state that social workers often do not understand the purpose of recording, resulting in them seeing recording as a chore. This means that they may not commit to the continuous development of their recording.

Case recording as a tool for good practice

Social work has always recognised the value of human interaction. Building relationships with people, based on empathy and respect, is fundamental to positive outcomes. Social workers require excellent verbal communication and interpersonal skills to gather, understand and appropriately share information. Recording is an important activity in all areas of social work. It takes up a significant amount of the working week, but it is one area we rarely consider in detail. We have never met a social worker who says that recording is their favourite aspect of the job and yet it is such a core aspect of every element of social work. In 1999, a manager quoted in 'Recording with Care: Inspections of Case Recording in Social Services Departments' said *"My staff are good at what they do, not what they write down"* (Goldsmith 1999). It is now recognised that recording (writing down!) is an essential aspect of social work and linking the 'doing' and 'recording' more closely together within the realm of 'practice' is essential. It is not unusual to hear the phrase 'if it's not written down then it didn't happen' in social work teams. We know that lots of social workers are irritated by this phrase. However, we do need to be clearer in our professional world about recording our actions and recognising the importance of this. Doing 'it' and recording 'it' are equally important in terms of social work practice, and recording should never be seen as an afterthought or chore.

Recording is especially vital in working with children and families and can hugely complement the work we do. Information needs to be captured and recorded accurately to ensure the best decisions are made for the child and their family. Lord Laming, in his inquiry into the death of Victoria Climbié, plainly states: *"the case file is the single most important tool available to social workers and their managers when making decisions as to how best to safeguard the welfare of children under their care"* (Laming, 2003: 6). Poor recording was cited as a significant factor which contributed to the tragic death of Victoria, aged only 7 years old.

It may appear obvious that we need to document what we do as social workers: we are accountable for our interventions, decisions and actions; we need to analyse information to inform robust planning; and we want to strongly represent the voices of children and families. Digging deeper into why recording is so important means that we need to explore the different stakeholders within social work practice.

What are my responsibilities as a social worker?

Social workers have an obligation to adhere to a range of ethics, values and practice standards, right from embarking on their studies through to becoming qualified professionals. Case recording, and protecting and sharing the information which is recorded, is central to our role. The Professional Capabilities Framework (PCF) underpins social work in England as 'one profession' across a range of specialisms and roles (BASW, 2018: 5). It could be argued that good quality case recording is an integral component to demonstrating competence and skills across all domains. Exemplary case recording will show professionalism, strong ethics and values, knowledge, critical reflection and analysis.

In relation to case recording specifically, Social Work England's (SWE) Professional Standards state:

"As a social worker I WILL:

3.11 Maintain clear, accurate, legible and up to date records, documenting how I arrive at my decisions (SWE, 2019: 8).

As a Social worker, I WILL NOT:

5.3 Falsify records or condone this by others" (SWE, 2019: 12).

Case recording should demonstrate clear purpose, evidence good practice, and highlight the impact of events on the child and their family. The British Association of Social Workers (BASW) is the UK's professional membership organisation for social work. Their 'Code of Ethics for Social Work' states the necessity for maintaining clear and accurate records:

"Social workers should maintain impartial and accurate records and clear evidence to support professional judgements. They should record only relevant matters, specify the source of information, distinguish between fact and opinion, and be prepared to be accountable for their record keeping."

(BASW, 2021: 11)

Why is recording important for children and families?

Recording is ultimately about the child's life. The key events, the highs and lows. We represent and advocate for the child's voice in our recording and share their views directly where possible, sometimes uploading their drawings and photographs too. This forms the basis of the work we do with children. It helps us reflect and consider what theoretical approaches would work best in the circumstances, what evidence base we need to move forward in terms of law, policy and research. It helps us plan alongside children and young people, to ensure their needs are fully met.

For children who become care experienced, this may be the only written record they can access which explains events and decision making. The records we keep may be the only source of seeing their early photographs and drawings, understanding childhood relationships and exploring what happened in their own childhood. Access to information can have a positive impact on the child's emotional wellbeing as they grow and develop, and well into adulthood, if they access their files later. Research with young people shows frustration that there are often gaps in personal information, and they have shared regret at *"how little personal information was stored such as photos and family mementos"* over time (Coram Voice, 2015: 15).

Pause for Reflection

Pause and reflect upon your own childhood experiences.

What personal information or 'records' do you have access to about your own childhood?

Why is this information important for you as a person?

How do you access your personal information or 'records' about your childhood?

The majority of us will have our own 'records' which will hugely vary from person to person. We might not call these 'records' in a formal sense, but we might collect and keep items which are important to us over time, such as birthday cards, photographs, achievements and reports, and other mementos. Many of us have family members or friends from childhood of whom we can share memories. Those of us who are parents ourselves, begin our child's 'records' often from the pre-birth stage and very early post-birth. We might save scan pictures, first outfits, toys or photographs. However, that's not the case for all children and young people. Social work recording, in this instance, can be life changing. Good recording can support therapeutic work, enhance life story work and help to heal trauma. Recording can provide answers to lifelong questions. It is very powerful. We have a huge responsibility to get recording right for all children, and especially care experienced children.

Family members often value written information, too. Sharing records of assessments and reports, for example, increases transparency and openness, and really enhances relationship building. Going one step further and writing records with families, rather than for families, in a collaborative and restorative way, reduces the power differential in what can often be a very uneven relationship. This can encourage, motivate and empower families. Working in this way means that what we record is not just an afterthought, but very much part of the relationship building process, alongside our interpersonal skills.

Chapters 4 and 7 consider case recording for those who are care experienced in more detail, including thoughts and advice from people who have had records written about them, delving further into why good quality recording is so important for children and their families.

Paul Yusuf McCormack was a care experienced artist and poet. Contributing to Maclean (2019) Yusuf shared a photograph of his case files, pointing out that 12mm represents 18 years of his life. Yusuf's book (McCormack, 2022) contains a powerful poem 'This Boy is Always in Trouble' which begins with the following reflection on his case notes.

The Boy is Always in Trouble (an extract)

My file:
Discoloured sheets of paper,
Lying randomly across one another,
Page numbers out of sequence,
No order; mixed up.
A contemptible file
Fashioned by those
Who claimed they cared.

My childhood life lies before me.
Gaps, gaps, I'm not complete.
Years have passed without any notes.
Did I even exist!
Didn't I mean something, anything, to anyone!
Was I that insignificant?

(McCormack, 2022: 123)

Why is recording important for social workers?

Although time consuming and, at times, frustrating in a busy social work role, recording really helps social workers to organise thought processes. We begin the necessary process of reflection and analysis, even in short recordings, such as those relating to phone calls and visits. We make decisions about what to write down and tease out the important aspects of a particular interaction. Recording helps us to decide what to do next, to make recommendations and plan next steps. Without the formality of recording, cases would easily drift, and things would get missed, as seen in many Safeguarding Children Practice Reviews and Serious Case Reviews. Recording helps social workers be focused, needs-led and strengths-based. It helps us to process our thoughts and manage our work more effectively.

Recording is essential for practical purposes, too. If we are unwell and not in work, colleagues can see what work is completed and what is still to do for a particular child and family. We have basic information, such as contact details, easily accessible for colleagues when required. We may need such information in a crisis situation and this needs to be readily available.

Why is recording important for other professionals?

Of course, all professionals need to keep records in some way, but this question is about why recording undertaken by social workers is important for other professionals. Case recording often becomes the basis for effective information sharing between professionals and organisations to identify need, complete assessment work, and to ultimately keep children safe (HM Government, 2018). We may share our written documents, and these need to be clear and accurate.

Our recording also forms the basis for decision making by others when we refer for outside services, attend forums or panels, or within the Court setting. These decision makers may never meet the child or family, and so they form their opinions primarily based on what we record. Therefore, good quality social work recording is vital to many other professionals.

Why is recording important for organisations?

Organisations, such as local authorities, have legislative responsibilities for the work they do with children and families. For example, for those children and young people who are care experienced, their local authority is also their corporate parent. There needs to be accountability and a way of measuring the work done, and this is often through recording. Recording also happens at higher levels of your own organisation. A team manager will record supervision with you as the allocated social worker for a particular family and will write key decisions made at the point of referral, at the end of assessment work, and as required when circumstances change. Higher managers in an organisation may read the records for a child and family, again, without ever meeting them, so it is vital that information is represented clearly, fairly and accurately.

For the organisation, recording provides:

- Evidence of practice to help plan, monitor and evaluate services
- A way of communicating so that there can be a continuity of service if the social worker is ill or unavailable for any other reason
- An increased likelihood of a smooth transition for a child and their family if a worker leaves or changes role
- Evidence of work and the basis on which key decisions have been made. This could be used in complaint investigations and as part of internal and external enquires
- Information to monitor, review and evaluate service delivery and the management of resources
- An audit trail for inspection.

The first ever care experience conference took place in Liverpool on 26th April 2019. The conference explored 'The care experience - past, present and future?' and brought together people of all ages with care experience.

The following image was created as part of a workshop at that conference. It presents a very powerful perspective on the key question of 'why?' in relation to record keeping.

Reproduced with the kind permission of the conference committee.

Other 'why' questions

We started this chapter by outlining how important it is to ask 'why?' In our experience as social work educators, sometimes students and others feel reluctant to ask 'why?', seeing it as a 'silly question' (remember there is no such thing!) However, unless you understand the 'why?' of something then you cannot fully understand the 'how'. In our experience 'why?' is often the most powerful question we can ask, certainly of ourselves. There are some other questions that start with 'why?' that are worth exploring in this chapter. The following why questions could help us to understand the barriers to effective recording.

Why do social workers struggle with recording?

Of course, not every social worker will struggle with record keeping, but most will say that they have struggled at points with the recording aspect of their role. Perhaps thinking through this question should start with your answer! Why do you struggle with recording? Generally, people talk about lack of time, problems with forms or data systems.

One of the difficulties that we see on a regular basis is that social workers do not schedule time in their diaries for record keeping. Perhaps this relates to the fact that workers sometimes resent recording and see it as keeping them away from their 'real job.' What then happens is that practitioners get behind with their records - or they end up doing them outside of their scheduled working time. You wouldn't cancel a visit or meeting without good reason, so why cancel scheduled time to complete case recording? Of course, we recognise crises happen and need prioritisation. It may be more sensible to respond during scheduled case recording time. However, if we perceived recording to be just as important as visits and meetings, we would make time in our diaries and stick to it, only cancelling when absolutely necessary.

Therefore, one of our main tips for record keeping would be to plan time in your diary. Most practitioners have an electronic diary, don't use this just to schedule visits and meetings. A key part of your work is recording, so schedule this into your diary, also. Where social workers get very behind with recording this can be overwhelming for them and can create a range of issues. A social worker was struck off for asking a third party to type case records, thereby failing to protect the privacy and confidentiality of the service users' and placing them at risk (Donovan, 2016). Think about when you might be most efficient and effective at case recording, which will save time in the long run. The beginning or end of every working day for a short period? In larger scheduled chunks of time throughout the week? Setting time aside straight after important visits or meetings? This may take some experimentation to see what works for you, but formal planning in your diary can be really helpful.

Why don't they teach us to complete forms at university?

Employers regularly comment that social workers are not effectively equipped for the role by their training (Mullan, 2014). The concerns that employers often have lie around the completion of agency documentation. Indeed, social work students have said to us 'we haven't covered how to do assessments'. In fact, what they mean is that they haven't covered how to complete specific assessment forms for a particular agency. Documentation will change over time, sometimes very regularly, and every organisation will have different paperwork for completion. Training someone at university to complete specific paperwork could actually be very unhelpful. Placements will give students the opportunity to experience the completion of agency documentation and professional training should provide some of the transferable skills required for record keeping.

Writing for social work practice, is very different from writing essays, although the skills used in essay writing, such as analysis, thinking about evidence, producing a structured document, writing for a particular audience, are the same skills used for social work practice. Rai (2014) notes that the types of writing required in social work practice, for example, report writing, case recording, and writing letters, all require different approaches, but each will draw on skills learnt through academic writing.

Why is consent and confidentiality important in case recording?

Informed consent should be gathered from adults with parental responsibility for all children and young people under the age of 16 years. Those aged 16 years or over will need to give their individual consent themselves. Consent, put simply, is giving permission to do something. Consent must be obtained in relation to seeking and sharing information from and to professionals in other services, as well as referring families to other agencies for assessment and provision of services. Agencies will have their own written consent forms, and usually accompanying explanatory leaflets, regarding gathering information. You should familiarise yourself with your own agency's form, and ensure written consent is uploaded or filed. If the child is of sufficient age and understanding, it is good practice to obtain their individual consent, too. The conversation relating to the agreement which has been reached can be written as a case note, making it clear to what the child or family member has consented.

Obtaining consent, both verbal and written, at the outset of the case does not mean consent has been obtained for every issue thereon in. Throughout your work with a family, you will be sharing what actions are required, and obtaining further consent on a regular basis.

There may be pieces of work or specific actions which require written consent. For example, if there is an agreement required between the local authority and the family, or if you need to obtain information about an adult in the family, such as their health information. Each referral to an outside agency will require specific consent. Recording consent, whether verbal or in writing, and the conversation which has taken place around this is very important, in line with data protection. However, there will be times when it is not appropriate to seek consent as it would:

- Place a person (the individual, family member, worker or a third party) at increased risk of harm
- Prejudice the prevention, detection or prosecution of a serious crime
- Lead to an unjustified delay in making enquiries about allegations of harm.

There will also be occasional situations in which consent of those with parental responsibility has been fully considered, and the decision is made to overrule this. It may be because the child, of sufficient age and understanding, has given consent themselves for a referral to a service, or parents or carers are withholding consent and this will impact on the safety and wellbeing of the child. You would always be discussing such complex, ethical dilemmas with your line manager and coming to an evidence-based conclusion with the decision recorded.

Why is it essential that our case recording is protected?

Any organisation which collects personal information needs to comply with the Data Protection Act 2018 which is the UK's implementation of the General Data Protection Regulation (GDPR). Data protection is essentially ensuring personal information is used fairly, properly and responsibly. It is about a person's fundamental right to privacy. On a practical level, ensuring data is fully protected builds trust between the individual and the organisation. Everyone responsible for using personal data has to follow strict rules, also known as 'data protection principles' to ensure information is:

- *"used fairly, lawfully and transparently*
- *used for specified, explicit purposes*
- *used in a way that is adequate, relevant and limited to only what is necessary*
- *accurate and, where necessary, kept up to date*
- *kept for no longer than is necessary*
- *handled in a way that ensures appropriate security, including protection against unlawful or unauthorised processing, access, loss, destruction or damage."*

(Information Commissioner's Office, 2021: 18)

Social workers must ensure that they are complying with all requirements, as mishandling or mis-use of information can have severe consequences. There have been instances where social workers have been sanctioned by the professional regulator, for example, in one case when a social worker sent sensitive client information to her personal email (Stevenson, 2017). It is your responsibility to ensure you are familiar with these requirements. However, you should receive training within your organisation in relation to the law and your obligations, before being asked to record or share information.

 Conclusion

In this chapter we have highlighted the responsibilities for social workers, as well as the importance of case recording for all stakeholders: children and families; social workers; our own and other organisations; and multi-agency professionals. We have asked you to consider what personal information is important to you from childhood, and how you access this. It is recognised that recording information is not straightforward and can be time consuming. We have asked you to reflect on what the challenges and barriers might be for social workers in a busy workplace, and given advice and guidance on what might practically help. Finally, we ask you to consider:

What have you taken from this chapter that will influence your case recording?

Why do you now think case recording is important? (Has your answer changed from considering this same question at the end of chapter 1?)

How will you use this knowledge with others, such as colleagues and within your teams?

 Talking it Through

It is always important to extend your learning and talking things through with others can be helpful. At the end of each chapter we include a link to a video showing some students and / or practitioners talking through the content and their learning. In this video Siobhan and Rebecca meet Jenna, a social work student and Kelly a newly qualified social worker in a Child and Adolescent Mental Health Team. They share their learning from the chapter and Kelly talks about her experiences with a recording task at university.

Chapter

3

Getting the Basics Right

Social workers obtain vast amounts of information on a daily basis, from a wide range of sources, and sometimes in very chaotic and challenging situations. Phone calls and emails are received and responded to, planned and unplanned home visits are made, children are visited in school, and meetings are attended. Emergencies regularly happen in-between. All of this information needs to be interpreted, processed and managed by the social worker. Decisions are made, both consciously and unconsciously, about what information to include and what to discount; where and how to record the information; and what words are used to describe events. These seemingly small decisions may appear unimportant and inconsequential, but they can have a profound impact on the relationship with the child and their family, and on how interventions are implemented by professionals around them. This chapter will provide some basic advice on how to record in social work. It is worth even the most experienced of practitioners revisiting these points on a regular basis.

Language matters

Words are powerful. Chosen well, words can empower and encourage. However, chosen carelessly, they can create stigma, barriers to understanding, or even cause offence. This does not help build a positive working relationship with children and families, or other professionals involved. When language is clear, strengths-based, and supportive, these relationships can flourish. Often the words we use in case recording have been emulated from colleagues, practice educators and managers, and the culture within our organisation. We rarely stop to fully consider the impact of our words on others.

Be jargon, abbreviation and acronym free and respectful in your choice of language

To clarify the terminology in this section:

- Jargon refers to words or expressions used by a professional or group that are difficult for others to understand.
- Abbreviations are words which are shortened. Indeed, the word abbreviation comes from the Latin word brevis meaning 'short'. For example, Jan is an abbreviation of January.
- An acronym is a word formed from the first letter of each word in a phrase, such as ASAP meaning 'as soon as possible' or PIN meaning 'personal identification number', often used in personal banking.

The world of social work, much like any other profession, has a language all of its own. This can create confusion, frustration and misinterpretation not only for children and families but also for professionals outside of social work. How often do we consider the words we use, and whether they are fully understood by others? How often do we see words and phrases in case recording such as 'engagement', 'resilience', 'attachment', 'good enough parenting', 'future risk of harm'? How are these words and phrases interpreted by children, young people and families? Such examples are subjective and offer little meaning, with social workers themselves struggling to agree on irrefutable definitions.

Different professionals can use the same language to mean different things. For example, social workers and some other professionals will see the acronym DV as meaning domestic violence, whilst nursery staff and health professionals may well see the same acronym as meaning diarrhoea and vomiting. This could create a dangerous confusion in terms of communication between the team around a child and their family.

Acronyms and abbreviations can also change over time, as services and terminology evolve. An acronym used 10 years ago, may have no current validity and be entirely meaningless. Without shared language and understanding, social work practice can become dangerous, and such discord can contribute to the imbalance of power between professionals and families. It creates the dynamic of 'us' and 'them'.

Pause for Reflection

Safeguarding Survivor (2018) is a blogger and parent, who has herself experienced care proceedings. She gives the following example of social work case recording, describing the use of social work jargon in general as 'divisive, demeaning and devoid of feeling':

"M was a LAC herself because of CSA / CSE and family breakdown, before she became a parent at 16. Her FC and LA felt the pregnancy destabilised the placement and placed her in a women's refuge after which her case was closed to the LA. During a later, difficult pregnancy (in which she became known to the perinatal MH team), M needed extra help; the LA held a TAF L1, which (after a MASH meeting) was later escalated to an L3, after which M's children became subject to S.17, and the CIN process. FGC not offered."

What are your initial observations?

Why is this case recording problematic?

How could you make the information more inclusive and respectful?

This extract is difficult even for a qualified social worker to understand, let alone another professional or family member. It feels cold, negative impersonal, and reduces the individual to a range of abbreviations and acronyms. There is a lack of context to the extract, and certainly no strengths identified. It feels very blaming of the young parent who has had a challenging life, for example, the phrase 'the pregnancy destabilised the placement' has a tone of criticism and reproach. This might be better worded as 'M's foster home was unable to meet her needs during her first pregnancy'. These subtle changes personalise the sentence, shifting the blame from the parent to the services being unable to accommodate her individual needs. The word 'placement' changed to 'foster home' comes across as less clinical and detached.

Children and young people who are care experienced, are trailblazing in challenging the words used to describe them and their personal circumstances. The organisation TACT have worked directly with children and young people to publish *Language that Cares*, which is a dictionary for social care professionals. Words, phrases and acronyms used regularly are challenged and replaced with preferable alternatives by these children and young people, for example:

Word or phrase	Young people prefer
Care leaver	*Care experienced adult*
Contact	*Making plans to see our family; Family meet up time / Family time; Seeing Dad / Mum / Grandma etc.*
Difficult to place	*Can't find a home good enough for them; Failed by the system*
LAC (Looked After Child)	*Call children by their names; LA should say 'our children' or [insert name of LA]'s children; Young People or Children*
Moving placements	*Moving to a new house; A new chapter or fresh start*
Peers	*Friends*
Siblings	*Our brothers and sisters; People who are related to me*

Adapted from: TACT (2019: 5-13)

A list such as this can never be exhaustive, nor suit every child and family, or every situation. Language evolves over time. The key is considering the words that you use in case recording, and the potential impact they may have on the child and their family. Being proactive in asking what words the families you are working with would prefer makes case recording inclusive and respectful.

Focus on the basics

Case files contain lots of factual information, such as names, dates and contact information, which needs thoroughly checking at the start of the referral process, and regularly as social work intervention progresses.

Families may have been known to your service previously, but this does not mean the information already recorded is correct. Often there are errors. Names may be spelt incorrectly, or addresses may be inaccurate. It is vital to recognise that inaccurate information can become 'fact' over time, when it is repeated in a variety of documents or reports. This is potentially very dangerous.

Other services who refer the family for social work support sometimes have the wrong basic information. Not taking care to check the accuracy of information can at best cause irritation for children and families and at worst cause offence, which does not assist in forming a positive working relationship with the family.

A person's basic details, such as their name, date of birth, address, school, family relationships, language spoken, ethnicity, and sexuality all form the basis of their identity. It can seem intrusive to ask lots of factual questions, especially when meeting a child and their family in the early stages of involvement. However, if you explain that you need to ensure the basic information is correct and that you are interested in how they define themselves, children and families usually respond positively. It shows they are valued and respected, and you want to make sure you get things right. If you are unsure of any detail, such as a person's ethnicity, first language or sexuality (if relevant), then ask them! It is best to record how the person views their own identity, rather than guessing or making the wrong assumptions, which can cause offence.

When working with a new child or young person, it is likely the first thing you will do is check the family's history within your service. If information has previously been entered incorrectly, the history may not be easily accessible. This means children's case files can be duplicated and need merging later down the line. This is frustrating and time consuming. It can also mean significant information is lost. A risk factor, such as a dangerous dog in the family home or an adult who poses a risk to the child, may be completely missed. This impacts on the social worker forming an accurate assessment of the situation, as well as potentially endangering the child or the professional visiting the home. Having all the relevant information ensures the social worker can plan safely when and how to make contact with the family. Does this need to be a joint visit with a colleague or professional already known to the family? Should the visit be announced or unannounced? Should the family be contacted by telephone? Is there time to send a letter with an appointment? Is an interpreter required?

Basic information is often used for statistical purposes. It may be used just within your own service, or it may be nationally collated to use for research and planning. Therefore, accurate information is needed to ensure services are evaluated and planned successfully.

Being factual

In relation to case recording, a fact is an event that has happened for which there is evidence; something which is known to exist; or information which can be attributed to a specific source. There may be conflicting information obtained in relation to events which occur from various sources. The key is to ensure the source of the information is clear.

Focus on Practice

It is easy for subjective words, with little factual meaning, to sneak into case recording:

'Roisin goes to school regularly'

'Trey's dad is a long-term drug user'

'Helena has missed a number of assessment sessions'.

What other information would you need to ensure the recording is accurate and clear?

Why are these examples problematic?

How would you improve these recordings?

The language used in all of these examples is vague and ambiguous, with very little meaning in relation to the impact on the child. These comments will be interpreted differently by a range of individuals, depending on their own personal experience and / or professional background. It is much better to use factual language and specific information where possible.

'Roisin goes to school regularly'

Schools often use percentages in relation to recording school attendance. This can be compared over time to see an improvement or a deterioration. Alternatively, saying a phrase like 'Roisin has missed school every Friday for the last 6 weeks' gives a clear pattern and timeframe. This helps to clarify and then explore what might be happening for Roisin on Fridays, and what can be implemented to support her.

'Trey's dad is a long-term drug user'

The words 'drugs', 'drug use' or 'substance misuse' conjure up a wide variety of images which are often very subjective. The terminology used to describe Trey's father in this example, defines him by a problem. This in itself is derogatory, negative and alienating for Trey and his father. There is no context or explanation for the substance misuse. There are no factual details which would help with assessing and analysing risk or enable the right level of support to be offered. Trey's father's views are not present. Did he report to the social worker himself that he was a 'drug user'? Is this an assumption made by the social worker? What evidence is this statement based on? Trey's father is also defined by being a father, and not as an individual in his own right.

Alternative wording could be:
'Simon (Trey's father) is a sole parent. He reports using cannabis every evening after work to help him sleep. This is after Trey goes to bed. He has used cannabis since his teens. Simon is employed as a retail assistant. He stated he spends approximately £25 per week on cannabis'.

'Simon is Trey's father and his primary carer. Simon states he uses cocaine socially when he goes out drinking with friends. This is 2-3 lines of cocaine every Friday night in town. He says he has never used cocaine in the family home, nor whilst caring for Trey, and does not feel this is problematic. Trey is cared for by Molly (paternal grandmother) every Friday night'.

The specific detail now included, gives a clearer picture of what is reported to be happening within the family, and what the potential impact of Simon's drug use might be on Trey. It is clear where the information has come from: in this case Simon himself.

'Helena has missed a number of assessment sessions'

In this example for Helena, it is unclear what assessment was being undertaken and for what purpose. How many sessions were offered, and how many missed? Is there any explanation for the missed appointments by Helena? Did the social worker make any adjustments to accommodate Helena's needs, if required? The statement appears judgemental and unbalanced. Perhaps something like the following could be more appropriate:

'Helena was offered 6 assessment sessions in relation to the parenting risk assessment for Court. Dates were given verbally and in writing to accommodate Helena's working hours: 3 sessions at the family home and 3 sessions at the social work office were planned. Helena attended 4 in total. Helena was unable to attend one session due to a hospital appointment for Ryan (child, 5 years) and she rang to give apologies. Helena did not give an explanation for the other missed session and was not contactable by phone on this date'.

This case note demonstrates Helena has in fact missed one session, not *'a number of sessions'*, without explanation. This gives a very different picture of the situation. It also demonstrates sessions were offered with Helena to accommodate her personal circumstances, and at different venues. It is an accurate account of what has actually happened. It is also fair to Helena, who has rung to give her apologies, and has attended the majority of her assessment sessions.

Focus on Practice

In light of these case examples, consider a piece of case recording you have completed yourself or one that you have read in a child's case file. Think about any positive changes you could make to ensure the record is clear, factual, fair and strengths based for the child, young person or family member.

What would you change or amend on the case record?

Why are these changes important?

How might these changes make a difference to the child, young person or family member?

Case notes first

It is tempting when completing a specific report or assessment, to avoid detailed case notes first, and write information straight into the report or assessment document. However, good practice would necessitate that each individual interaction with the family is written separately as a unique case note. This can be considered by social workers as duplication or timewasting. However, information can be forgotten, missed or inadvertently changed if not recorded as a case note first. It is easy to begin to write your hypothesis and analyse information without fully considering it, which can become dangerous practice.

Focus on Practice

Case record by Heidi Bloom (social worker, East team 6)

23.4.2019 at 9.30am: Debbie Tyndell (Learning Mentor, First Lane School) telephoned to inform me that Daniel is not in school today and his mother's phone is switched off.

Case record by Heidi Bloom (social worker, East team 6)

23.4.2019 at 11.00am: Jane (mother) and Daniel (child, 6 years) were present during today's unannounced home visit. Daniel was not in school and it was initially reported by Jane that he had a temperature and therefore she did not send him. I observed the curtains closed, and there were 2 empty bottles of wine on the floor. Jane was wearing pyjamas and stated she had slept on the settee. When asked about her alcohol use, Jane admitted to drinking both bottles of wine yesterday from 4pm and into the evening. Jane said she feels her alcohol use has become problematic. She said she was unable to get up to take Daniel to school today, but sometimes Daniel refuses to go anyway. Daniel said he had played on his computer all morning but had not eaten any breakfast yet. He said, 'I'm hungry'. Jane immediately got up and prepared some toast for Daniel. There was food observed in the fridge and cupboards. Daniel was dressed in joggers and a T-shirt. These were clean and age appropriate.

What are your initial observations?

Why are individual case notes useful?

How would you improve this recording?

The case notes above are recorded with the exact time and date the interactions occurred. It is clear who spoke to whom, and what their relationship is to the child. We know the home visit was unannounced. There is a clear description of what the social worker observed, and what Daniel and his mother said directly to the social worker.

However, rather than recording the interactions separately, Heidi (social worker) decided to put this information straight into her assessment as we can read in the following example.

Focus on Practice

Excerpt from Heidi's assessment:

Daniel's mother has an alcohol dependency problem. She regularly drinks in the evenings, and this impacts on her ability to get up and take Daniel to school. Daniel is missing school. There have been times when Daniel has not had food at home and has stated he is hungry. The home conditions are poor.

What are your initial observations?

Why does the assessment differ when individual case notes are not analysed first?

How would you improve this recording?

In this excerpt, the information has become very generalised, with little detail or evidence base. The social worker has made the assumption that Jane is alcohol dependent, when Jane actually said she feels her alcohol use is 'problematic'. This is a very different interpretation, and Jane may feel not listened to and upset by this. The social worker has assessed the home conditions as 'poor' but has not provided an insight into what this actually looks like, or how it affects Daniel. Poor home conditions have different connotations for different professionals, and this is far too vague. It is unclear when Daniel is missing school, and the assumption has been made this is definitely due to Jane's alcohol use, which again is not necessarily accurate. The social worker has not included the strengths within the family to be built upon, which are highlighted in her case notes. For example, Jane having food in the family home; Jane being open about her alcohol use; and Daniel's clothing being clean and age appropriate.

Pause for Reflection

Thinking about the excerpt from Heidi's assessment consider:

What impact might this have on planning for the family?

How might Jane and Daniel feel reading the assessment?

Why is accuracy, strengths-based practice and fairness so important in case recording?

When assumptions are made or information is not thoroughly analysed, the social worker may recommend actions which do not tackle the core issues. This means that any plan made is likely to be unsuccessful in the long term. This is frustrating for the child, their family, and all professionals involved. It can lead to disengagement by the family, and they can be labelled 'hard to reach' 'hostile' or 'challenging'. Forming the wrong conclusions in an assessment will ultimately lead to forming the wrong plan for the family. This is not only wasting the time for all involved, but likely to use valuable resources or services which were unnecessary in the first place.

Neither Jane nor Daniel will feel listened to by the social worker. They have shared important information which has been bypassed. Jane acknowledged she is struggling with her alcohol use, which may be a significant step for her, and this was misinterpreted. Jane could feel upset, angry, disillusioned, or resentful towards the social worker. This could impact on her ability to be open and honest in future. Without highlighting strengths, the family may feel attacked and criticised. They may feel unmotivated and apathetic in making changes. These issues will inevitably impact on the social worker's relationship with the family.

 Conclusion

We recognise in this chapter that *"writing is not a neutral act"* and social workers need to be conscious of the context in which they are working in and the impact that they have (Dyke, 2019: 56). The language we use is hugely important for relationship building with children and families, and we have given examples from children and young people themselves, which they consider inclusive and child-centred. We have explored why the basic information we obtain is integral to good quality case recording and have considered the impact that inaccurate case recording can have on engagement, analysis and planning, and ultimately on outcomes for children and young people. We hope the examples used in this chapter have sparked reflection and can influence good practice in your own case recording. Finally, we ask you to think about:

What you have learned from this chapter?

Why are the 'basics' so important in good quality case recording?

How will this influence your own case recording?

 Talking it Through

It is always important to extend your learning and talking things through with others can be helpful. At the end of each chapter we include a link to a video showing some students and / or practitioners talking through the content and their learning. In this video Siobhan and Rebecca meet with Nicola, a newly independent social worker. Nicola has dyslexia, dyspraxia and Irlen syndrome. Nicola shares her learning from this chapter and also discusses her experiences as a neurodivergent social worker keeping records.

Chapter

4

Keeping the Voice of Children and Families Central

In this book, we have tried to take what might be described as a 'belt and braces' approach to keeping the views of children and young people central. Throughout the book, we have included thoughts from people who have had records written about them because, when developing skills in recording, it is important to focus on the needs of the people the recording is about. We decided to also add an extra chapter focused solely on the views of people who have experienced recording practice in children's social care and to place this centrally in the text in order to model the vital importance of having the voice of the child and family central in all record keeping. Did you notice that the usual circle with the chapter number in has been changed to a heart? This is to illustrate the fact that the voice of children and families should be at the very heart of your recording.

An open letter to the social worker who wrote my case notes

Whilst we were finishing this guide, we read an open letter from Rebekah Pierre to her social worker. This linked so closely to what we are trying to convey in this book that we approached Rebekah and asked her if we could include the letter in this book. She very generously agreed and explained the reason behind the letter.

"When I accessed my care-files as an adult, it was difficult to comprehend how and why I could have been written about with so little respect. I felt powerless, silenced - like my social worker's version of events, committed forever to a digital archive, took precedence over my own. I felt I needed to have the final say. The following is an open letter I published in response, containing extracts of my care files."

Dear Trace

Before I wrote this letter, I double checked the spelling of your name just to make sure it was correct. I know how jarring it can be when the basics are not quite right; you misspelt my name almost one hundred times in the case files you wrote about me whilst I was under your care. I received these last week, after submitting an SAR request to the relevant local authority.

Speaking of names, let me remind you of mine. My name is Rebekah. It is the Hebrew spelling, and I am quite fond of it. It may sound like a small detail to some, but to me, it matters. It is the name I was given when I was born.

Case 1

O Notice of other agency
contact with child / young
person

Further details

Rebekah telephoned (this is the spelling of her name according to her). She stated she is

I once corrected the spelling, as you can see in case note 1. But it never was changed on the system. Instead, a rather blunt note was written to say 'this is the spelling of her name according to her' (for the record, I wasn't lying). This was just one of many examples where I was not believed.

I don't know if my name rings a bell - but even if it does, you probably wouldn't recognise me now. You were involved in my life at a time I was extremely vulnerable and on the verge of being homeless - a 16-year-old girl with everything to live for, who didn't have much interest in living at all.

Case note 2

Identity

Child / young person's needs	Actions / services	Additional services	Frequency / length	Person / agency responsible	Start date	Planned outcomes	End date	Actual outcome
Rebecca is a young perosn who appears a little mixed up about the direction of her life and the influences around her.								

Family and social relationships

Since that time, much has changed; despite being a 'young person who is a little mixed up about the direction of her life' (your words - see case note 2), I ended up following in your footsteps. I wanted to be like the residential social worker I had after you, who practised with care, kindness and compassion. I have since had the privilege of practising alongside many such practitioners, who transform lives every day. On reflection, perhaps I wasn't so 'mixed up' about the direction of my life after all?

During my career, I have read case notes of varying quality. Most have been child-centred and thorough. Others have not. But for all I have read, nothing could have prepared me for reading my own records - particularly the entries written by you.

To give you the benefit of the doubt, I imagine you have changed since writing these records. Your approach may well be unrecognisable now; it is why I took the time to write this letter. I have some small faith that this time, you will hear me. I hope in earnest that you will.

I cannot pretend my recording is perfect. I know how hard it is to write good case notes whilst balancing competing deadlines and crises. But I have always done my utmost to be respectful - to write with the child in mind.

In your defence, I don't think I was the audience you had in mind when you wrote them, was I? Perhaps you saw the screen in front of you as the final destination. It was not; your words, written about but without me, would not remain hidden forever. One day, I would understand my rights.

Speaking of rights, do you remember taking me to an Achieving Best Evidence interview after school, where I had to disclose the most traumatic events of my life to yourself and a police officer? It was my right to have an advocate - something I only learned years later.

It took all the strength I had to get through those 4 hours, with no emotional support or break. I have never felt so small, so humiliated. Looking back, it was like an inquisition. Like somehow, I was the one on trial. Now it is my turn to ask the questions.

The first is this; how dare you?

Case note 3

The allegations she has made against☐☐☐☐☐are complex. It appears that they started experimenting at the age of ☐ and ☐ respectively and that a 'relationship' has been on going. It is unclear as to whether there was violence, aggression or coersion. It is also unclear in relation to consent issues - further interviews are required.

It took more courage than you will ever know to disclose that a child known to my extended family, who became an adult whilst I was still a minor, abused me throughout childhood. If you believed I was 'experimenting' or in a 'relationship' with the perpetrator as you suggest in case note 3, then your thinking isn't only flawed, but dangerous. I was a child. I could not consent.

I refer you to the independent inquiry into CSE in Rotherham - something you would have known about, given this was then ongoing. Its messages are clear: Do not blame victims. Show empathy. Believe them.

Which begs the question - where did you draw the conclusions that the allegations were 'complex' with 'consent issues'? What observable evidence did you base this on?

Were you there when the perpetrator threatened me into silence, forbidding me to tell anyone? Did you feel the weight of this threat, a terrible yoke around my neck?

Were you there when I used to crawl under the bed to hide from them? Did you hear as I made my breathing imperceptible so I wouldn't be found? When I played dead to survive?

Were you there in the room when it happened? Did you watch as my soul left my body, a pattern of dissociation which continued long after it stopped?

Were you there when my OCD spiralled out of control? When I couldn't pay attention at school because, in my helplessness, I used to repeat the same 5 words incessantly in my mind for hours on end? Please-God-Make-This-Stop?

Were you there?

Case note 4

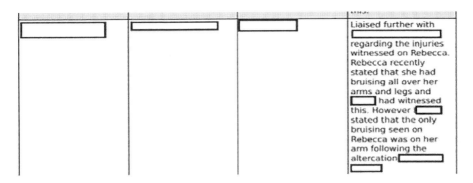

Liaised further with
regarding the injuries witnessed on Rebecca. Rebecca recently stated that she had bruising all over her arms and legs and had witnessed this. However stated that the only bruising seen on Rebecca was on her arm following the altercation

This was not the only time I was not believed. When disclosing domestic abuse, the marks still fresh on my body, you minimised this too.

Is an attack on a child at the hands of an adult ever an 'altercation' as you describe in case note 4, or is it abuse? And why were you so concerned that bruises were 'only' seen on my arms? Does the absence of one (and by the way, bruises fade) negate the other?

Case note 5

Rebecca presented at A & E on the 17/11/09

EDT Only

☐ Request for Appropriate Adult

Action taken

☐ Provision of information / advice   ☐ Referral to other agency

☐ Passed on as referral   ☑ No further action

On a similar note, why, after I presented A&E dangerously unwell, was 'no further action' recommended, with no explanation? Do you know how it feels to read that such a traumatic event was met with a tick-box?

Case Note 6

The above called with concerns relating to ▮▮▮▮▮ following an argument with ▮▮▮▮▮ in Skegness.

Both children had stated that they were scared to return ▮▮▮▮▮

▮▮▮▮▮▮▮▮▮▮▮▮▮▮▮▮▮▮▮▮▮▮▮▮▮▮▮▮▮▮▮▮

Advised that Rebecca could return home to her flat in ▮▮▮▮ due to her age and level of independence.

No further action seems to be the common response, as seen in case note 5. After I called you in distress 200 miles away from my unregulated placement, you advised I could return alone due to my 'age and independence'. No follow up was ever given to see if I was okay.

Case Note 7

22.45. Rebecca contacted EDT from the ▮▮▮▮ were she is currently residing.. She stated she felt ▮▮▮▮ was being physically abused by ▮▮▮▮

She was on the telephone today to ▮▮▮▮ somehow ▮▮▮▮ thought the phone call was over, but Rebecca states she could hear ▮▮▮▮ shouting at ▮▮▮▮ This conversation is partly recorded according to Rebecca. She then states that she saw ▮▮▮▮ who said ▮▮▮▮ had punched ▮ in the face. Rebecca would like to talk to her social worker.

My records, just like your involvement with me, ends rather abruptly. The very last sentence stands unanswered across the passage of time. I never did hear from you again.

It is too late to go back in time. But it is not too late to make a meaningful change for other children. May your words be worthy of each of them. Who knows, one day, you may find yourself reading what they grow up to write about you.

Yours,
Rebekah (with a k)

Rebekah's letter with the extracts from her case notes is very hard hitting. It shows very clearly the importance of good recording. Working through the chapters of this book and thinking about the basics of good recording practice should help you to record in ways that are much more appropriate than Rebekah's experiences.

Social workers who have care experience, like Rebekah, understand record keeping from different perspectives and therefore their reflections can be particularly valuable. In the book 'Insiders Outsiders: Hidden Narratives of Care Experienced Social Workers' (Carter and Maclean 2022) Jo Thompson's reflection 'A page to fill' provides some important advice for social workers. Jo has kindly given us permission to include an extract from her reflection in this book:

A Page to Fill by Jo Thompson (an extract)

"One day last year I received an email containing my files from children's services. I was shocked that my past just showed up in my inbox. I think I had expected to be forewarned, maybe offered a meeting? Isn't that how it works? Damn. I should know this stuff! I'm a social worker! I should know how this works! If this was an adoption file, I would have had a meeting, someone to sit with me and look at the files. Instead, I sat at my kitchen table, with these emails glaring back at me. Too much to send in one email – this is exciting and daunting in equal measure. I opened the files early one morning, close to Christmas, with my husband next to me. He is there, my anchor, holding me still as I enter this potential storm.

It's hard to say what was the biggest shock, my Mum's vehement rejection of me, the disdain directed towards my parents by professionals, or the lack of a child-centred approach in this 1970's system. Astonishingly, in the whole file, there is actually very little about the children, practically nothing about my older siblings. It's really all just about my parents, and about professionals trying to manage these two very unwell people.

My older siblings have talked about some aspects of it, and they too were 'Received into care' a number of times. But they were children themselves, and their memories and perspectives were that of children. I know now that I have seen the information, they knew little of the reality of what was taking place.

As an adoption social worker, I know the importance of your story, your history and identity. So why had I left it until my forties to seek this information? Fear of what I might find out, upsetting my parents, my siblings......myself? I have never identified myself as a care experienced social worker. On panels, or training or anywhere. Why? Because I didn't know my story. I didn't know what to say had happened. I couldn't tell, because I didn't know.

I was eventually returned to my parents care on a permanent basis and there were no more social workers.....but there were still problems.....and with the knowledge I have now, I am intrigued by the decision that I was returned and left in the care of 2 adults with such profound mental health problems. I am surprised that for the duration of my childhood, my parents were left to parent me.....or I was left to parent them.

There have been many improvements in the way information is recorded, and I have some thoughts and suggestions from the experience of reading my files and also reading files of children I currently support.

I would urge social workers to write details about the child. We repeatedly document concerning incidents and themes on files and forms, and this is important. We also record in detail about what the parent did / said. The child will want to know about the situation in relation to them. Where were they when the concerning incident happened? What did they say and how were they afterwards? Describe what they were doing when you visited them at home, what toys they played with and if they interacted with their siblings. This is the kind of information they may never get from another source. Help them know what they were like and who they were.

Demonstrate curiosity in your recording, such as 'I wonder how the child felt when...' This shows that you were holding the child in mind, that they were important and that their wellbeing was the absolute driving reason for your involvement and actions. When reading my file, it very much felt like my parents were the clients, and not, in fact the children. A child's daily life is heavily documented once in foster care, let's give them more information about the time with their birth family.

I acknowledge the challenge in doing this when we need to so carefully record details of the concerns, and ensure we gather sufficient evidence. So many of the documents we use do not lend themselves to child centred recording. Approaches are used which are a step in the right direction for file recording, but there is room for further development.

Ultimately though, I am extremely grateful for those recordings, and for the laws that mean they were retained. Without this, a huge part of my identity would still be missing. Some of the file was so incredibly hard to read, and there are parts I wish I could unknow. But finally, I have my story. I can tell it – should I choose to. That means more to me than anything."

David Grimm's Top Tips

David is a final year social work student. He was a member of the Social Work Student Connect Team and also a member of the Association of Care Experienced Social Care Workers. David was a member of the 'Love Group' of the Scottish Care Review and is also proud to be a friend to care experienced people around the world.

David is an incredibly talented artist and poet (although he wouldn't necessarily say this of himself). He created the image on the back cover of this book. He also created the sketch at the end of this chapter which really summarises the content in a visual form!

Based on David's experiences reading his own case files and witnessing the impact reading case files has had on his friends, David has put together the following tips for social workers who are record keeping in children and families social work:

A few tips for record writing:

1. The person you are writing about should be at the fore of your mind at all times. Whether you're considering applicable theories or legislation, their relationship to a long-lost grandparent or even simply just stating how challenging you're finding the work with said person, they should always take priority, this will allow for a more personable written piece and helps remove any sense of alienation, when the person asks to read those records later on in life.

2. Names are everything, get them right from spelling to context, for some people under the care of social work, their name is literally the only thing they have left, they have no family, no possessions or money and are left with just their name, respect it.

If that's not a compelling enough argument, it's a human right under the United Nations convention on the rights of the child (article 7) *"the child shall be registered immediately...right from birth to a name"* (unicef.org.uk, 2022).

It is not OK to put a sibling's name where the person's name should be. Such a small mistake to you but can make the reading of your records that much harder, I kept thinking that not one person had cared for me (I know this to be untrue) but if they couldn't get my name correct then how could they care. It's a huge deal.

3. Consider how your writing will be perceived. You may feel like these will only be seen by professionals who will understand your rash, bold and borderline offensive language choices as well as your more balanced choices. But when your words are read by the people you are writing about...let's just say that the old rhyme about sticks and stones breaking bones and names not hurting was so wrong, so very wrong. Everything from word choice to tone (imagine how you've felt when you've had an email that is dry and left you second guessing). Receiving records is difficult enough, receiving rushed, disorganised and messy information from someone who is your carer / guardian etc. cuts deep and can present barriers to consuming the knowledge they were seeking in the first place.

4. Be clear in your meaning. Depending on where the person lives, they don't need to be an adult to access their care records, imagine how devastating it might be to misunderstand the tone (sorry to reiterate this point), of your social worker's reports about you, but equally how uplifting and reassuring it might be to read something clear and, where possible, positive about your interactions. Please never be scared to write down how proud and impressed you are when it happens, this positivity can last forever in a young person's mind.

Being a child / teenager is terrifying enough without finding out that your carers are describing you as a troublesome attention seeker or a person with an overzealous need to be loved (paraphrasing of course but language choice is paramount).

5. Do your best (your genuine best) to not copy and paste. It's so clear when this has been done, and yes there are times when nothing has changed but at least take the time to write that, take the time to show you've reflected on the person "nothing has changed since

I last saw Jane / John, they appear to be OK / not OK" taking a moment to show an original thought can mean the world.

6. If you're going to redact a document or part of a document (writing down information that you know will need to be redacted is barbaric in my opinion) at least check it is done properly. The process of reading a document that's been redacted can be a jarring thing to undergo, it brought back severe paranoia and caused me to really worry about the information that was hidden, whereas other friends had names visible that were supposed to be legally hidden (such as abusers). So double check, you would check your court reports so check this too!

7. In a similar vein to previous tips. Records are horrific to read, very important but difficult, stressful, and horrible...consider writing to the person that's reading them. Letter writing records is becoming increasingly popular and I can see why.

8. Be human in a bureaucratic environment. Be yourself, stick to your driving values and always consider how you'd like to be treated / written about and you will be an amazing record writer.

We are very grateful that David has been generous enough to take the time to both write something and to draw something for inclusion in this book. David has also joined us in discussing this chapter and his thoughts about recording which is included as the video at the end of this chapter. Along with David, we are also joined by Mary Carter.

Mary Carter is a social worker who has lived experienced of the care system. Mary qualified as a social worker in 2020 at the start of the global pandemic and not long after receiving the prestigious award of student social worker of the year in 2019. Mary works with children and families as a social worker. She also sits on fostering and adoption panels for a local authority and independent fostering agencies. In addition, Mary leads skills for fostering training and presents as a guest speaker for various organisations such as secondary schools and independent fostering agencies. Mary wrote the following reflection to support readers of this book to think carefully about what they record.

It's not what you wrote about me, it's how you made me feel. By Mary Carter.

'That's not my life, that's not my story, who even am I?' These were the words going round and round my head when I received the first part of my file. The file that was left unsealed, the file that was so "complex" that I couldn't receive it all together. Am I complex, is my file complex or is printing it complex? I still do not know. The only place I would be able to find any answers, really understand my past and hope to make sense of my muddled memories was in my Social Care file, yet down to the "complexity" I had to wait a significant amount of time until I received the next part, (oh along with a gentle email reminder from me each time chasing for them to be sent). Imagine reading your life from an envelope in a series of parts all mixed and not in chronological order. It appears that I wasn't important, my journey wasn't important, matching the narrative I carried through most of my teenage years.

Untangling myself from the file is something that has never left me, that I am still coping with and for someone who loves to write with freedom, makes writing these words actually quite a challenge. Who is Mary Carter? I am still learning. Just writing these few hundred words, I fall into a freeze, in terms of my emotional response. Some would call this a trauma response which it is, but so much more than that too; shame, stigma and pure embarrassment, which I continue to carry. While reading case notes from my file to help me put this contribution together, I sat with my partner, a man and probably the only person I truly trust who also knows about my lived experiences, I couldn't even read the full account to him because of the emotions it aroused in me.

I would love to start a family in time, where do I even begin with my story with my children when I still cannot make sense of it myself? I cannot make sense of it as they are not my words, they do not reflect what I felt at the time, they reflect the significant power social workers hold over children and how the social worker decides what the child knows, thinks and feels. In my practice I write with an understanding that the child will one day read their file. I explain things to them before I even consider pushing buttons on my laptop so that they will really see, hear, feel and understand my words. Within my own file are incidents, events, people that I cannot even recall as no one spoke to me, no one helped me understand or capture the all important "voice of the child."

Language is power, the words we use personally and professionally reflect and affect a person's world. Those that know me and work with me know how much I care about the words, phrases and talk we use in social care. As a result of reading my own file, my attention to detail in what I write in case notes is ever so much more important and ever so much more compassionate.

I am still to come to terms with the impersonal language written by social workers who I cannot even recall. This person has so much power in my life, yet I do not remember who it was that said, "given her mental state at this time she should not be thinking about studying Psychology at college." How an earth do they have the right to decide what I study? What professional qualification did they have to determine this? Should they not of been thinking in the opposite way, empowering me to consider a course that would help me to understand my traumatic and frightening childhood? I would like to think that in my practice, children and their families will always remember me due to the relationship-based style in which I work and the way I ensure they are present in my recording.

Revisiting the title that "It's not what you wrote about me it's how you made me feel," you made me feel terrible and now I feel even worse as I can see what you said and thought about me, yet never told me. This is not social work, this is insensitive and oppressive.

At the end of every case note is a frightened child, desperate to be heard and understood. As social workers let us harness the power of language.

 ## Conclusion

We have tried to keep the voices of children and families who use social care services central in every chapter of this book. However, we decided to also have a chapter focused solely on the views of social workers who have had records written about them. They are in a unique position to reflect on record keeping practice. The following image drawn by David Grimm is perhaps the best conclusion for this chapter:

What is the key message for you in this chapter?

Why do you think the social workers in this chapter feel the way they do?

How might you record differently as a result of reading the contributions in this chapter?

 Talking it Through

It is always important to extend your learning and talking things through with others can be helpful. In the video accompanying this chapter Siobhan and Rebecca meet with David a care experienced social work student and Mary a care experienced social worker who works in a children and families assessment team. Dave and Mary wrote the two final contributions to this chapter, and they share some of their thoughts with Siobhan and Rebecca who reflect on their learning from reading and compiling the chapter. This is the longest of all the videos at the end of the chapters because we didn't want to cut any of what Dave and Mary shared. There is a great deal of learning to reflect on from this video.

How to Record Home Visits

The 'social analysis' which is central to social work, often takes place in the family home (Trevithick, 2012: 7). The home visit offers insight into people's lives and social surroundings and requires social workers to develop a different range of skills. Despite home visits being the most common place for social work to take place, Ferguson (2016: 67) notes the complexity of home visiting, which has been largely ignored in research, yet "*constitutes a distinct sphere of practice and experience in its own right*". Ferguson further highlights that:

"*The daily experience of family life is fluid and lively as adults and children interact, play, eat, cry, fight, the TV is on, their mobile phones ring or ping, the dog(s) bark, growl, demand attention or other distractions such as adults whose identities are often unknown to social workers are present.*"

(Ferguson, 2016: 69)

When things go seriously wrong and children are harmed within families, it is often said the child was 'invisible'. We will consider this further in Chapter 9 which focuses on lessons learned from Child Safeguarding Practice Reviews and Serious Case Reviews. However, it must be remembered a child becoming invisible in such cases, should not be reduced purely to 'bad practice'. Ferguson states invisibility needs to be understood:

"*in terms of the interaction of organisational processes, the practitioner's qualities, their visceral experience and emotional state during face-to-face encounters, and the atmospheres within which the practice occurs.*"

(Ferguson, 2016: 1021)

To capture all this multifaceted information using your full range of senses is a real challenge. In the UK, social workers often carry out core aspects of their work, including home visits alone. They are often *"navigating their own emotions and biases"* and making judgements based *"only on their recollections"* (Ferguson et al, 2020, in MacAllister, 2022: 72). What did you see, hear, smell or touch on the home visit? What are the key elements to record? What information do you now discard? Undertaking and recording the home visit is a truly complex activity.

Working in collaboration with families

There is no better opportunity to understand the child's world than spending time in their home (Nicolas, 2015). Many professionals do not have the opportunity to see the child's living environment and observe family relationships in such an intimate and personal way, therefore social workers are in a unique and privileged position. Building relationships with the child and their family is essential to high quality social work. As Featherstone and colleagues assert: *"where practitioners seek to work reflectively with the family and establish shared understanding of their encounters, family members recounted they are able to invest more actively in the working relationship"* (Featherstone et al, 2018: 75). This demonstrates the importance of the social worker being able to listen attentively, display respectfulness, empathy and honesty, and recognise strengths within the family during the home visit. The child and family should be able to read the case recording and recognise it to be an accurate account of the interaction which took place, including a true interpretation of their views.

Social Work England's Professional Standards begin with promoting the rights, strengths and wellbeing of people, families and communities, stating that social workers will *"work in partnership with people to promote their well-being and achieve best outcomes, recognising them as experts in their own lives"* (SWE, 2020). Ensure the home visit, where possible, is conducted in collaboration with children and their families. This can include consideration of the time to visit which takes into account the family's commitments, encourages a shared agenda, and genuinely values their contribution.

Personal safety

Keeping safe and minimising any personal risk will enable you to focus all of your attention on the home visit (Nicolas, 2015), thus enabling collaborative working and supporting quality case recording. Before you embark on a home visit, be sure to check there is no information within your own service or from other professionals working with the family, which indicates there may be a risk to your own safety and wellbeing. Risks to a social worker could be in relation to a specific member of the family, their wider network, family pets or within the local community.

Pay attention to your own senses, which need to be on high alert, during the visit (Nicolas, 2015). The social worker's own emotions will undoubtably influence interactions, as home visits can evoke feelings of anxiety, excitement, sadness, hope, despair and fear, to name but a few. How you feel should assist in assessing the level of risk to the child. For example, if you feel threatened or fearful, how might the child feel living in this household? What can you smell in the home, such as illicit substances, cigarette smoke, alcohol, urine or faeces? What impact do the living conditions you observe have on the child? Also be mindful of a home which appears well presented too. Have you seen other areas of this home? Is this a true reflection of the living environment?

Ensuring your own personal safety and wellbeing is not a one-off event, but an ongoing process. Family circumstances and risks to workers can change from visit to visit.

What is the purpose of this visit?

Home visits can be announced, where are family are expecting the social worker to visit, or unannounced, where the social worker attends without prior warning to the family. In either circumstance, the social worker does not always know what will present to them when they arrive. Therefore, in addition to excellent observational and communication skills, there is also a need to be flexible and creative on the day. 'Routine' home visits can feel "*mundane and unremarkable*", yet they are still "*routinely alive with the possibilities of the unknown, full of complex challenges and emotions and sometimes drama*" (Ferguson, 2016: 71). The worker's ability to reflect both 'in action', at the time the event is happening, and reflect 'on action', after the event has taken place, will also influence what information is processed and collated (Schön, 1983).

Reflection for action in preparing for the home visit should begin long before the social worker walks into the child's home. Formal planning, including risk assessment and considering exactly what information or work is required, takes place between the social worker and their manager and / or colleagues, usually back at the office, with informal planning taking place on the way to the visit by the worker alone (Ferguson, 2016). Even if planning is only for a few minutes, for example in the case of emergency home visits, it will help to clarify the information required and reduce the worker's anxiety, thus having a positive impact on interactions. Having a clear plan also assists in taking good quality contemporaneous notes during the visit (if appropriate), and transferring information onto the child's file later, aiding thorough reflection and analysis. Recording the right information, which is concise and analytical, will ultimately save time in typing later on. Win-win!

Focus on Practice

Think about a visit you are going to do either in your own social work practice or hypothetically as part of a university case study. Consider the following questions in your planning for the home visit:

- Are there any documents you need to read, or any professionals you need to liaise with before this visit takes place?
- Do the family need an interpreter, advocate, or family member to support them?
- Do you need a colleague to visit with you? Reflect on why you feel a colleague is needed and how would they support the visit? What is your role and what is their role? Are there any downsides to having a colleague accompany you?

- Why exactly are you visiting the family? (Think about narrowing down the reasons for the visit to the specific child and their family rather than saying 'to undertake a statutory visit').
- Who in the family do you hope to engage with and why? Have you considered the practicalities of how you might achieve this?
- Is there new or specific information to be shared with the family? If so, how will this be shared - verbally or in writing? Is it appropriate for the children to be present? How will the family's views on the new information be collated and recorded?
- What will you do if there are unexpected adults or children present when you arrive? (Consider confidentiality, as well as how you might practically manage this situation).
- How will you ensure that the child is seen alone, or their interactions with caregivers are observed? How will you make sure their voice is heard in the subsequent case recording?
- Are there any checks (such as observing specific rooms, sleeping arrangements, home safety or the child's access to food) which need to be completed within the family home during this visit? How will you explain the reasons for these checks to the family?
- How can you ensure a shared plan / agenda for the visit alongside the family?
- How will you record the information today? Are you (or your colleague) able to take notes during the visit or is the plan to make notes on key points immediately following the visit, in the car or back at the office?

These considerations will help you feel more focused and confident on the home visit and will support good quality case recording during and after the visit.

It is always helpful to write a brief plan, based on these reflective questions, before you go into the house, especially if the visit has the potential to be disordered or chaotic. Always try and have a shared agenda with the family. What is important for them to discuss or work on during this visit?

Actions should always be proportionate to the concerns raised, which again is why purposeful planning is so important. Always ensure you are clear what the concerns are. An investigation into child sexual abuse may not warrant looking in the fridge or cupboards for food; however, if there are concerns regarding neglect, it may be necessary *"to look under the bed for food, beyond sweet wrappers, check the state of the child's bedding and look in the kitchen cupboards and the fridge for food"* (Nicholson, 2015: 1). Actions need to be balanced with respecting the family's privacy, and always trying to promote a positive working relationship. If you are clear why you need to take a specific action, this can be explored fully with the family, thus aiding partnership.

Be open with the family about the purpose of the visit and what you hope to achieve. If you need to check your written plan, at any stage of the visit, again just tell the family what you are doing. They are likely to value your thorough consideration of their visit and respect your professionalism. Equally if the visit has not gone according to your written plan, it can be helpful to compare the initial objectives to what actually happened. This can aid systematic reflection and analysis. Why was it not possible to achieve your aims today? What factors influenced the change of direction? What were the barriers? What did you achieve instead? What needs to happen next?

To take notes or not to take notes?

Using pen and paper, or typing notes on a laptop, during a home visit can create a physical barrier to the family's engagement. That is not to say notes should not be taken contemporaneously. It all depends on the nature of the visit, your relationship with the family, and your professional judgement regarding the pros and cons of note taking in a specific scenario.

You may choose to take notes on an initial visit following a new referral. There will be information you need to record factually, such as the details of people living in the household (including accurate spellings and dates of birth), extended family members' details, or professionals and agencies working with the family, including addresses and telephone numbers. These details would be very hard to remember without a written note. Clearly, if the home visit is planned to conduct an assessment session, note taking would be necessary, to ensure you accurately record the family member's views within the context of the questions you ask. However, there will be many home visits where note taking feels inappropriate or even oppressive.

Words of pain, hurt, betrayal and violence are shared with professionals on a daily basis, and families need to be heard (Featherstone et al, 2018). A child or parent may begin to disengage if you decide to take notes during an emotional encounter, either feeling that you are not interested in their story or they may feel uneasy about the words you choose to write. Actively listening and being present with child or adult is the most important social work skill at these emotive times. You should make your notes following the home visit, as soon as practically possible, so that the service user's words are not lost, and to ensure the information is recorded accurately.

In relation to a child making a report of physical abuse, emotional abuse, sexual abuse or neglect, unquestionably the information should be written down as soon as you can. This is always in the child's own words, with the question posed to them (if any), and then signed and dated by yourself. This initial written document can be scanned and uploaded directly to the social work system, and a formal record typed to accompany this. However always keep the original document in a safe place, even if it is scrawled on the back of envelope! The handwritten note may need to be shared with the Police if a criminal investigation is pursued, or even presented as evidence in Court at a later date.

What should be included in the final written record?

Home visits are influenced by national and local procedures, including what information should be gathered on an initial home visit, and within specific statutory guidelines, such as for children subject to child protection plans. Once again, make sure you are familiar with your own local procedures and guidance on what basic information should be gathered within home visits, and where these details are to be recorded.

The very basics are essential as always. For example, the exact address visited, the time and date of the visit, and who was present. Remember the child should always be seen alone, where possible (HM Government, 2018).

Focus on Practice

The following is an example of a case recording for a home visit for a 5-year-old child.

Name of child(ren): Daria Ball

Name of parent or carer: Simone Ball (mother) and Asa Richardson (father)

Place of visit: 22 Fairfield Drive, Kitchley (home address)

Time and date of visit: 4:00pm-4:45pm on the 28th February.

Who was present at the visit? Daria and Simone were present. Asa was at work.

Observations:
Simone was aware of my visit, as I had rung her at 10am today to arrange. She knew I had received information from the Police regarding a domestic dispute at the property 2 nights ago from our telephone call. Daria had witnessed this incident.

Daria answered the door and was keen to show me a sticker she had received from school which said 'fabulous phonics'. I asked Daria about her day at school, and she appeared happy and chatty. Simone showed me into the living room, but I noticed she closed the kitchen door very quickly. I asked to see Simone alone first to share the Police information. Simone asked Daria to go upstairs to her bedroom to play for a few minutes. I read the Police report to Simone, which stated there had been a verbal dispute on the 21st February, and the neighbour had rung the Police. Daria had been present. I observed the living area to be clean and tidy. The room was warm. There was a colouring book and some pens on the rug on the floor. I shared the Police information - see Simone's views below.

I asked why Simone had been keen to shut the kitchen door. She appeared apprehensive and looked at the floor, but said it was because Asa had punched the door and there was a mark on the other side of it. I asked to observe this. There was a hole in the door halfway up. The kitchen was very cluttered, with take away cartons, used tins of food and dirty plates and cups all over the work surfaces. The floor felt sticky, and there was a smell of cigarette smoke, even though the window was slightly open. Simone said she had not had time to clean up today as she had been busy. She appeared very tired with dark circles under her eyes and she looked like she had been crying. I asked how she was feeling today and she shrugged and said 'ok'.

Child's views:
Daria was seen alone in her bedroom. This was well presented. She had matching curtains and bedding, and a range of toys. She was playing with plastic toy figures on the floor.

I asked Daria about her sticker from school. She was very animated and said she had done good reading with her teacher. She also told me she played outside with her friend, Harvey, after school 'for a bit'. I said to Daria that the Police had told me about an argument at the house, and Daria nodded, but looked down at her toys and went quiet. I asked if she was ok. Daria said 'mummy was shouting at daddy and daddy hit the door. He hurt his hand and went to nanna's'. I asked how Daria had felt, and she said 'sad' and again looked down. Daria added 'mummy was sad, but she cuddled me in my bed'. Daria then asked me to play with her toy figures and I asked no further questions. She was really engaged in her play.

Parents' views:

Simone shared the argument happened as Asa spend the last £30 at the bookies. Simone said "I was so mad, I just started shouting at him". Simone said she knew this had scared Daria, as she came down from her bedroom and then Asa went into the kitchen and started punching the door. He cut his knuckles. He left the house and went to his mother's home. Simone said she felt upset as Daria "looked really scared". Daria didn't want to sleep in her own bed and I got in with her for the night. Simone said Daria didn't want to go to school the next day, and they were late attending because Daria had cried a lot, she added "she seemed ok today though and had a good day". Simone said Asa returned to the house yesterday and was really sorry. He said he'd had a drink with his mate after work and they went to the bookies together, and didn't mean to spend the money. Simone said she's worried Asa is struggling at the minute, and he's drinking and gambling more. Simone said it was really loud shouting during the incident and said "I don't blame the neighbours for ringing the Police". Simone said Asa would be back from work at 7pm today.

Analysis:

Simone was open about the incident and shared what had happened and showed me the damage to the door when I asked. She let me see Daria alone. The information shared by Daria and Simone was consistent with the Police report. Daria was clearly scared by the incident and struggled to sleep that night, and this impacted on her school attendance. The conditions of the kitchen have deteriorated since the last visit, as the home is usually very clean and well presented. This is out of character for the family. Simone seemed very low in mood today.

Actions:

- To talk to Asa about the incident, gather his views, and ask about current alcohol use and gambling

- To inform school of the incident so they can support Daria if she becomes upset and explain the reason for her late attendance yesterday.
- To explore with Simone her own mental health and wellbeing at the next visit.

Next visit:

10th March at 3.30pm

Signature:

Amelie Bond (senior social worker)

This is one example of a home visit for a young child, and there will be elements of the style or wording you may not use yourself, and parts you think could be improved. Writing is an individual activity. However, we will consider the strengths of this recording.

It is logically written, and evidences who was seen, where and when. The child has been spoken to alone and her wishes and feelings documented. The content is very much factual, with either observations by the social worker or information shared directly by the family recorded in 'observations', 'parents views' and 'child's views'. The social worker had a clear purpose and plan for this visit, which was openly shared with the mother during the telephone call beforehand.

The social worker used her observational skills during the visit. She challenged appropriately and respectfully when she noted the door to the kitchen was closed. The social worker has written quotes in quotation marks to make clear these are the exact words of the family. There is clear reflection on the visit to give a strong analysis, which has informed the 'actions' which are now needed. Overall, the record is set out well and is accessible. It has subheadings which make the record easy to read.

The home visit in context

We have focused largely on planning, undertaking and recording individual home visits for children and their families so far in this chapter, however it useful to consider how home visits need to be considered in context. In their triennial report of serious case reviews taking place between 2014 and 2017, Brandon et al (2020) found in the majority of the cases relating to neglect, the incidents were dealt with in isolation. Different workers may become involved as emergencies occurred, or in the event of staff sickness, and over longer periods there may be changes in lead worker for the child and family. Being able to look back and understand case recordings is essential to avoid drift. Brandon et al (2008: 1) coined the term 'start again syndrome' to describe, primarily in cases of neglect, the poor analysis of past history and parenting capacity, which offer the same interventions time and time again, without critical reflection on the impact for the child.

Case recordings, especially of home visits and direct interactions with the child in their own home, may be reviewed long after they are written and can be critical in offering a timely and accurate intervention for the child. Good quality record keeping and communication of relevant issues and incidents with other agencies is necessary to provide a clear picture of the child's life, identifying patterns, concerns, strengths and unmet needs (Brandon et al, 2020). This links to having a good quality chronology in the child's file, running alongside day-to-day recordings and interactions.

 Conclusion

In this chapter, home visits have been considered in detail. The chapter highlights the complexity of undertaking home visits, often alone. However we acknowledge the privileged position we are in as social workers, accessing a family's personal space in often very emotive circumstances. We have emphasised how challenging the home visit can be, and highlighted tips for ensuring personal safety, planning ahead and considering the purpose of the visit beforehand. All of this will assist in helping us feel focused and confident during the home visit, having a direct impact on good case recording during and afterwards. We hope the example recording of the home visit helped you to think about what good practice looks like. We ask you to ponder the following questions:

What have you taken from this chapter which will help you case record home visits well?

Why do you think these considerations have an impact on what you write in your case recordings after a home visit?

How will you use this learning in practice?

 ## Talking it Through

It is always important to extend your learning and talking things through with others can be helpful. At the end of each chapter we include a link to a video showing some students and / or practitioners talking through the content and their learning. In this video Siobhan and Rebecca meet again with Jenna, a social work student and Becky a social worker with children with disabilities. They share their learning from the chapter and also their experiences in undertaking home visits.

How to Record Social Work Meetings

Meetings between professionals and family members at key decision-making points are embedded within children's social work in the UK (What Works for Children's Social Care, 2019a). As a student or newly qualified social worker, you will have no doubt have been asked to 'minute' or record a meeting for a colleague, perhaps without any specific guidance on how to do this in practice. The ability to accurately and efficiently record the information shared, and the outcome and actions from a meeting is an essential skill in social work. This is directly linked to good practice, as how the information is recorded and the words you use, can have a bearing on decisions which are made, and how the family responds. Once again, the focus needs to be strengths-based, balanced and achieving desirable outcomes for children and families.

What meetings will I record?

There are a wide range of meetings which take place, which the social worker or social work team manager is predominantly responsible in leading or 'chairing', and then subsequently recording and distributing the information within a set timescale to relevant family members and professionals. These meetings can include:

- Child in need meetings
- Child protection core groups
- Risk and vulnerability management meetings (in respect of a child who is at risk of child sexual exploitation, child criminal exploitation or going missing)
- Public Law Outline (PLO) meetings

- Personal Education Plan (PEP) meetings for a child looked after
- Pathway planning meetings for young people leaving care
- Professionals meetings

There may be additional meetings specific to your organisation, or similar meetings with different names, which regularly take place.

Meetings which are recorded by social workers are predominantly held directly with the child (of sufficient age and understanding); their family; and a range of relevant multi-agency colleagues. They can be small meetings, perhaps with one parent and a couple of professionals. However, they can be large meetings, usually if there are multiple children, complex family dynamics, or situations warranting the involvement of many professionals, such as for a child with complex health needs.

It's all in the planning

It may sound unusual to consider the planning of the meeting when exploring how to write comprehensive and accurate notes. You may feel planning is irrelevant and unnecessary when it comes to completing the written record, as you will ultimately record what is discussed anyway, irrespective of the preparation. However, a meeting which is carefully planned will not only run more smoothly but will be more focused and therefore easier to record.

Research exploring how to effectively engage families in decision making meetings, found three core stages were necessary: pre-meeting preparation; the process of the meeting; and effective follow-up. This study concluded that preparation and follow up were 'at least' as important as the meeting itself (What Works for Children's Social Care, 2019a: 4). Three 'high level', interconnected mechanisms operated across all stages of effective decision-making meetings, whether 'statutory' child protection or more voluntary 'child in need' meetings, and these were:

a. *"Enabling collaboration and engagement*: creating a meaningful dialogue between professionals and family members;

b. *Building trust and reducing shame*: Building trust between social workers and families is an important mechanism for parents and the wider family to feel able to participate in a meeting in a way that is open, and solution focused;

c. *Enabling participation in decision-making*: To enable families to be involved in making important decisions about the care and safety of the child. This involves in depth preparation, and everyone being willing to listen and be flexible."

(What Works for Children's Social Care, 2019a: 5)

Strengths-based and non-judgemental language used in verbal and written communication in preparation for the meeting itself, helps the family actively participate and build meaningful relationships, alongside professionals. The venue, time and date are significant. A venue which is easy to reach and well known to the family will immediately make them feel more relaxed. They will be able to get there with little complication, which in turn minimises stress and anxiety.

Consideration needs to be given to the commitments of the family. Plenty of notice, where possible, will ensure the family are able to have a discussion with the social worker, regarding the meeting's purpose and the expectation of attendees. Families will be able to consider their own childcare needs, especially for younger children, who may require attention during a meeting and prevent the family from fully participating. Families will be able to make arrangements for older children to be taken to or collected from school, if it is not appropriate for them to attend. As a social worker, you need to explore if the meeting can take place around the adults' work hours, other appointments and commitments, and around the children's school and nursery routine.

Ask yourself what support can I offer the family for them to fully participate? This could also include advocacy, interpreting services, or a family or friend to be present to offer emotional support, or assisting with childcare. Helping a family feel fully included, with their needs considered, will minimise unnecessary conflict or disengagement before and during the meeting. This in turn is helpful to be able to achieve comprehensive recording.

Pause for Reflection

Before a meeting takes place, it is useful for you to consider the following questions:

Does the child, young person and / or family understand the purpose of the meeting?

Is the meeting linked to the outcome of my assessment? Therefore, has the assessment, analysis and recommendations been shared with all relevant parties?

Have I obtained explicit consent to share information in the meeting from the child or young person (considering their age and understanding) or from those with parental responsibility?

Have I explained who is invited to attend the meeting? And why?

How will I ensure the child, young person's or family members' views are fully represented?

How will I organise the meeting? Have I considered the practicalities of this meeting, such as venue, time, and any additional support required?

If a child, young person or family member chooses not to attend, how will I ensure their views are represented?

Have I planned a post meeting de-brief with the child, young person or family member to ensure they fully understand what has been agreed, and have the opportunity to share any concerns they may have?

Is the family clear how long it is anticipated the meeting will take? Does this impact on a parent's ability to manage their childcare or access public transport?

(Adapted from Moray Council, no date)

The power of circles

The arrangement of the room can have a direct impact on how a family engages in the meeting. An environment which feels like a boardroom is cold and intimidating, increasing the sense of powerlessness for families. Sitting around a table can feel very formal, which may be necessary or even unavoidable for some venues, however sitting in an open circle may be much, more productive and empowering. If you think creatively about the meetings you lead, you'll be amazed at the outcomes!

Often linked to restorative practice, the use of circles has flourished in areas such as education and the criminal justice system to assist in building and maintaining relationships, and repairing harm (Leeds City Council, 2021). Circles can represent continuity, wholeness, inclusion, unity and equality. Conducting social work meetings in a circle can have a profound impact on participation and outcomes for families as it encourages active listening, without the distraction of laptops, phones and notepads, which can act as a barrier. Circles reduce the power differential between professionals and family members, as each participant is seen as equal. When considering case recording, however, there is the dilemma of note taking during the meeting, which is essential to ensure an accurate record is made.

Pause for Reflection

If your organisation is not familiar with restorative practice or using circles as the basis of meetings and you need to develop confidence in this area, you could initially try using circles with colleagues. This could be within team meetings, internal training sessions or group supervision. It can feel a little alien at first! Consider some reflective questions:

What were the key differences from meetings you usually attend?

Why do circles make a difference?

How did it feel as a participant or the facilitator to hold a meeting in a circle?

There are a number of practical and innovative ways to record meetings, and you may be able to think of more within your service. You could ask a colleague to take notes on your behalf, and sit outside of the circle to do so, to ensure minimal distraction for those taking part. You may be in a position to record the meeting using video or audio equipment, with the permission of all participants of course. This would require careful consideration regarding storage, and how this information would be used. For example, would the audio or visual recording be destroyed once notes have been typed onto the social work system? Would you link the recording directly to the child's case file? How would the outcome of the meeting be captured for participants? Would they be provided with a copy of the recording? With advancements in technology, these may be everyday methods in the near future.

A simple, collaborative and transparent way to record notes when circles form the basis of a meeting, is by using flipchart, a smartboard or white board. All participants can visually see what is being written as the meeting is happening. The social work role is that of facilitator: keeping focus and leading the discussion. You could use relevant phrases, questions or pictures as headings to capture key information. Ask the child, young person or family member to write the information themselves during the meeting if they feel able or ask what words they would like you to write on their behalf. Before the meeting happens, you could work with the family to decide the headings, or even support a young person or parent to be the facilitator. This is their meeting! You can refer to this throughout the meeting as needed, and it will really help when you summarise information and come to decision making. The key outcomes and plan going forwards can be highlighted, again visually, for all participants to see.

The information can then be transcribed, or photographs of the information uploaded onto the social work computer system. Just be mindful to ensure someone unfamiliar with the case or someone who has not attended the meeting, are able to fully understand the discussions and outcomes. Therefore, additional information may need to be recorded when the meeting is formally written up and distributed.

Chairing effectively

Writing notes during a meeting, whether chairing at the same time or as an assigned note taker, is a challenging task. Invariably, participants do not form an orderly queue to say clear and concise sentences, one after the other, in a coherent and logical format. They will perhaps talk over each other, go off on a tangent, remain silent and say very little, or have lengthy, drawn-out views. Therefore, it is difficult to ensure all the information is written down accurately, and in a thoughtful and balanced way. If you are taking notes for a colleague, you will be reliant on them to chair the meeting well. This means following a logical structure or format and displaying the key skills of a good chair: attentiveness, decisiveness, flexibility, assertiveness and diplomacy. As note taker, you need to be clear of the purpose of the meeting yourself, and clarify what the chair expects from you beforehand. You will usually have the added responsibility for typing up the information, as your notes and any shorthand you use, is unique to you.

It could be argued that it is not possible to chair any meeting brilliantly and write comprehensive notes at the same time. However, for social workers, in a time of austerity and limited resources, this is often the expectation in practice. You could be the allocated social worker for this family, therefore sharing your own information, facilitating the meeting, and be note taker, all rolled into one. This does pose some clear practice challenges. Formal chairs of meetings are usually impartial and focus on facilitation only. However, in this scenario you are clearly an active participant. Therefore, to exert control, manage conflict, encourage quieter participants, think on your feet, and actively listen, whilst writing notes, takes a great deal of skill and practice.

It is imperative you have a plan or agenda, and ideally enable the family to set their own agenda (What Works for Children's Social Care, 2019b). You could write the meeting plan on a flipchart for all to see, or give each person an individual copy. For more complex meetings, you may even request information is shared by each professional with the family prior to the meeting taking place, and / or a short written report submitted a few days beforehand. This is the process for attendees at Child Protection Case Conferences and can be easily replicated for other meetings you are asked to lead. It is helpful to have the minutes of the previous meeting, where relevant, and the child's current plan with you, to make sure tasks have been completed. These basic methods will help keep the meeting on task, and there will be no surprises for the family. Most meetings will follow this simple 3-part process, and this will also form the basis of the final case recording:

1. Introductions and purpose of the meeting
2. Information sharing
3. Action plan or review of the plan

Have a mechanism for all participants to sign into the meeting with their name, relationship to the child and full contact details. This could be a simple signing in sheet as people enter the room or passed between participants at the start of the meeting. This will ensure you have up-to-date information, including spellings of names, when recording the meeting. It will also ensure any formal record after the meeting is being distributed to the right email or postal address. Make sure you agree a review meeting time and date, if this is required, when everyone is present, as it will save on organisational time later on.

Final recording of the meeting

Not all meetings will be recorded in the same way. There may be specific templates or proformas within your organisation for various meetings which you are required to use, or you may be able to decide how the information is ultimately written down yourself. The final case recording will link back to the purpose of the meeting, who will receive copies, and how the information is to be used. Does the information need to be recorded verbatim, be a brief summary or reorganised into relevant headings? Will the meeting recording be required for a decision-making forum or for Court? Does it need to be recorded in a specific way to ensure the family fully understand the content? Case recording of meetings will have a varied audience, including the child or young person, and their family, as well as professionals who know the family well, and some professionals who have perhaps never met them. Writing for multiple recipients is a challenge and does need careful consideration.

Focus on Practice

The following paragraphs are an excerpt of the discussion from the first child in need meeting regarding Abdul (8 years). He lives with his mother, Aliyah, and father, Suliman.

Child in need meeting for Abdul Patel

Attendees
Sarah (Social Worker)
Ben Holden (Team Manager)
Derren Tasker (School)
Yasmin Rhodes-Sinclair (Family Support Worker)
Aliyah

Apologies
Suliman (dad)

Discussion
An assessment was completed and this recommended a child in need plan for Abdul.

Abdul is displaying challenging behaviour at school and at home. In the past he has ran out of the family home, and gone missing for 2 hours. Abdul has seen his mum and dad arguing. The Police have been called by neighbours 3 times in the last 3 months. School said he is not doing very well academically, and doesn't concentrate well. He has missed a lot of school this year and is nearly always late. Aliyah said Abdul won't go to bed when she tells him to, and they don't always have bus fares. Suliman is not always at home for bedtime as he works night shifts. Abdul has poor eye sight and has broken his glasses. Abdul gets frustrated when he can't see his school work properly, due to his eye sight. The School Nurse said Abdul is up to date with his immunisations, but needs a dentist.

Suliman wasn't at the meeting today. He was in bed because he finished work at 7am. Aliyah came alone, but didn't say too much. Sarah (social worker) has visited Abdul at home and he said he likes to play computer games in the evening. He doesn't have any friends at home and he said his mum shouts a lot at him, and he is scared when his mum and dad argue. Sarah has also met Suliman.

What are your initial thoughts on this recording?

Why is this recording, in parts, problematic?

How would you improve the recording?

This excerpt is very jumbled and a little vague. The title should include Abdul's date of birth, and when, where and the time the meeting took place. Information regarding the attendees needs improvement, ensuring their full names, job role or relationship to the child, and their organisation is clear. The school nurse is mentioned as sharing information, but her details are not recorded as an attendee. Therefore, was she present, or was this information given to the social worker before the meeting? It is unclear. Parents names will ideally be listed first. They are key participants and central to the meeting.

It would be useful to record why an assessment was completed for Abdul for the other professionals present or anyone reading the document unfamiliar with this family, given this is the first child in need meeting. This should be central to the discussion in the first child in need meeting. A short summary of the strengths and areas for support identified by the assessment is needed, before going into information from other participants. Key headings would break down the information clearly, making it easier to read for the recipient. In this example, you would perhaps write information under the name of each professional in attendance or separate the information into topics such as 'health', 'education' and 'social work update'. There may be times a meeting needs to be recorded as the conversation happens. Always ensure there is a section for the child's views and parents views. This is especially important where they disagree with information or have a different account.

Be clear exactly who said what and when events happened. Record the information factually and precisely. When exactly did Abdul go missing for 2 hours? The phrase 'in the past' is very unclear. In relation to Abdul's eyesight, was it the school staff member who said his eyesight was 'poor', the social worker or the school nurse? What does 'poor' actually mean? Ensure the information is precise, so say exactly how much school Abdul has missed this year, and how many days he has been late. The meeting should focus on Abdul's needs, so what is the impact of all these issues on him?

There are a few sentences which could be further clarified, such as 'challenging behaviour'. What does this mean for Abdul, and are there examples of how Abdul does respond well in school, ensuring a balanced view? Finally, this excerpt comes across as very negative, especially in relation to the parents' contribution. Aliyah did attend but did not appear empowered to share her views fully. Suliman was not present, but the social worker stated she had met him, so what did Suliman say about the current situation and support the family need? In relation to Abdul himself, did he say anything positive about his family? What does he like or enjoy?

This case recording would not empower parents to make changes or engage in support. They may feel upset, not listened to, and perhaps angry receiving these minutes. It does not present as a balanced recording, given the piece states a full assessment has been completed by the social worker. Always make sure recordings are balanced and the strengths are highlighted.

Extended family and community support has not been explored here. There may be more strengths to be highlighted. Suliman is in employment, which is positive, but this comes across as negative in the recording.

The plan

A critical activity for social workers is making plans (Wilkins, 2016). All children in need, especially those in need of protection, children looked after, and those leaving care, must have a care plan. Many children with disabilities will have an Education, Health and Care Plan (EHCP). Writing plans is so common it becomes a routine part of the role, and the recording of this is not often analytically considered. Plans should be devised in collaboration with children and families, or even better, with families through Family Group Conferencing, for example (Wilkins, 2016). The importance of developing plans is explicit throughout Working Together (2018), which states:

"Social workers, their managers and other practitioners should be mindful of the requirement to understand the level of need and risk in, or faced by, a family from the child's perspective and plan accordingly, understanding both protective and risk factors the child is facing."

(HM Government, 2018: 28)

The vast majority of meetings will have a plan for the child and family to work towards. Plans can hugely differ, depending on the family's circumstances and current level of social work intervention. However, all plans, irrespective of these factors, should be Specific, Measurable, Attainable, Relevant, and Timely (or SMART using the acronym!) Before explaining this further, it is important to highlight, as Wilkins asserts, that simply writing a plan based on these principles is unlikely to make the difference:

"the key is to incorporate these principles into your thinking, discussions and co-productions with families so that, as a natural result of the process, better care plans are produced."

(Wilkins, 2016: 6)

The most important part of the planning process is involving children and families. If they feel empowered and connected to their plan, they will be more engaged and committed to the actions needed with support from professionals and their support network.

Focus on Practice

To ensure plans are SMART, we will consider each aspect individually:

Specific - *What is expected? Why? Who is involved? Where should it happen? What might be the requirements and constraints?*

Measurable - *How much? How many? How will we know if it is achieved?*

Attainable - *Is this realistic? How can this be achieved?*

Relevant - *Does this seem worthwhile? Is it the right time to do this? Will this achieve an improved outcome for the child?*

Timely - *When does this need to be done by? Consider the child's timeframe and the level of risk associated.*

(Adapted from Meyer, 2003, in Wilkins, 2016)

Take a reflective review of plans which have been completed in your team for children and their families. This could be an individual or whole team exercise to consider how your plans could be improved. Put yourself in the shoes of the child and their family who are the centre of the plan.

What are your observations of this plan? Is the plan SMART?

Why is SMART planning so important?

How could you make the plan SMART-er?

The plan is the key part of the meeting. This is what the family are working towards, with the support of professionals. They need to understand the expectations of them, and the expectations of those around them, to ensure accountability. The plan will not only be used to refer to, but to review progress based on clear outcomes, and it is therefore not just a case record, but a practical, working document.

The wording of the plan needs careful deliberation to be strengths-based, outcome-focused and achievable. Carefully considered wording can empower the family and help them feel they are ready and able to make changes in their lives. Have clear, attainable outcomes or goals. What do the family themselves want to achieve? Are the outcomes or goals written in a way that it will be clear when changes have been made? Try, where possible, to write outcomes or goals in the words of the child and / or family. This is their plan after all! Families will have their own ideas on what they want to achieve and how this can be done. Through working with the family closely, goals with professionals will be more aligned. Using the family's own words is a powerful way for them to own their plan and understand what the actions mean to them. It helps the family know what they are expected to do and what support they will be offered along the journey. Plans can be amended and adapted along the way. Plans are adaptable and flexible, responding to changes and any new needs or risks.

Finally, ensure the plan is concise. A family will feel overwhelmed if there are too many points to the plan, or too many areas to focus on. Remember, the plan can be staggered or tiered, perhaps focusing on the three to four most pressing changes required for the child then, once these are addressed, the plan can be amended to include other tasks. Thus, building on the positive changes the family have already made in a strengths-based way.

Focus on Practice

Consider the following plan for Abdul. How would you feel as Abdul's parents? How could this plan be improved?

Child in Need Plan for Abdul (8 years)

Goals

For Abdul to go to school every day and not be late.

Abdul to go to bed at a reasonable time.

Aliyah and Suliman not to argue.

How will these goals be achieved?

Aliyah and Suliman will ensure Abdul gets to school on time every day, and ring school if he is absent to explain the reason. School to monitor.

Aliyah and Suliman will make sure Abdul is in bed for 8pm on school nights.

Aliyah to go on a parenting course. Suliman can attend this course if it fits in with his work commitments. Please note there is a 2 month waiting list.

Social work visits at least every 20 working days in line with organisational procedures. Abdul will be seen alone and his wishes and feelings gathered.

Review

To be reviewed on 19th November (8 weeks time)

Starting with the goals: these are essentially the measure of the plan working or not. Depending on how much school Abdul has missed and how often he is late, the first goal may not be completely achievable. Perhaps a goal which states 'Abdul's attendance and lateness to significantly improve' or 'Abdul's attendance to increase from 65% to 85% for this academic year' would be more attainable. Abdul to go to bed at a reasonable time, would hopefully positively impact on his lateness and school attendance. The word 'reasonable' is vague, but a specific bedtime has been clarified in the plan. The final goal stating 'Aliyah and Suliman not to argue' is not a child centred outcome, nor is it realistic for parents never to argue. The goals should always focus on the child and be about the impact on the child. An alternative goal could be 'Abdul not to feel scared through experiencing arguments between his parents' or 'Abdul not to experience loud arguments between his parents as this makes him feel scared'. Abdul has said to the social worker during her assessment, that he feels scared when his parents argue, so this is a good word to use within the goal. These are the direct words of the child. You can play around with the wording of goals or outcomes and see what works for the family you are supporting.

The plan here does not really say how the family are to be supported by professionals involved. There are clear expectations on parents, with not much support in place to help them. How will Aliyah and Suliman be supported to get Abdul to school every day and on time, and how can they ensure he goes to bed at 8pm when this has not happened so far? Aliyah has already stated she struggles when Suliman is at work in the evenings. This plan sets the family up to fail. There may need to be steps taken or support put in place as first steps. For example, the family support worker could undertake a piece of work with Abdul and his parents to explore the bedtime routine and look at what would help them get Abdul to bed by 8pm. The social worker could explore the family finances, as to why they don't always have bus fares. You could consider if work is required in respect of budgeting or debt management. Finally, what is causing the couple to argue? This may be linked to some of the issues already identified, or some areas the couple need to work through. Again, what steps are needed to help Aliyah and Suliman reduce their arguments? Perhaps a referral to couple's counselling or creating some time for parents to speak together about their relationship, away from Abdul.

It is unclear what specific parenting work the couple require, and the point on the plan which states 'Aliyah to attend a parenting course' is ambiguous. You would want both parents to be following the same advice, so a course suitable for both Suliman and Aliyah together would be beneficial. There is no consideration of support before the parenting course commences, given the 2-month delay. The family may feel this is too long and be disheartened before the plan has even started. There could be some individual work completed in the meantime as preparation for the course, and to build confidence for parents to attend a group work setting. There are no timescales on the plan. You would need to make sure there are timeframes for each point, and which professional or family member is responsible for the action. There are a lot of considerations to ensure plans are SMART, and that they really support the child and family to make long term, sustainable changes.

Other considerations

There may be rare circumstances in which a parent or carer with parental responsibility is formally excluded from a meeting. This can occur if they pose a risk to the child, to other family members attending, or to professionals. There may be a specific Court order in place, such as a restraining order or non-molestation order, which prevents two individuals having direct contact with each other in such a setting. A parent may even be imprisoned. In these circumstances, careful consideration will need to be given as to how the excluded family member can participate in the meeting, where possible. This can include requesting written information from the person before the meeting happens, or for a professional to meet with them directly and share views on their behalf. If a decision is made not to inform them at all, due to the level of risk this may pose, then this decision will need to be formally recorded on the child's case file. This is usually completed by the team manager making it explicit why this decision was taken. You may have formal guidance within your organisation on this matter, or need to seek advice.

There are occasions when a 'professionals meeting' may be necessary to consider a complex family situation and devise a way forward. This would not include family members. The family may be made aware of this meeting taking place beforehand, and the outcome of the meeting afterwards. However, in some cases, such as a strategy meeting to decide if enquiries need to be made under section 47 of the Children Act 1989 (child suffering or likely to suffer significant harm), it may be that the family are completely unaware of the meeting taking place. This is because knowledge of the meeting may increase risk to the child or jeopardise a criminal investigation. If the minutes of a meeting are requested by the family, and they have not been in attendance, again a decision will need to be recorded in the event they cannot have a copy. In meetings without the family's attendance, always record information as though they were present and listening, ensuring respectfulness throughout.

There will be other meetings that social workers attend as a participant, and the written record is completed by another professional or an administrator assigned for the task. This can include:

- Family Group Conferences
- Initial Child Protection Conferences and Review Child Protection Conferences
- Child Looked After (CLA) reviews
- Fostering or Adoption panel
- Internal panels within your organisation, such as those to seek permission to instigate proceedings or to pursue specific advice and guidance.

For these meetings, you will receive a written record which you may be responsible for checking in terms of accuracy, and possibly filing or uploading to the child's case record. You will need to consider if there is significant information to be recorded on your social work system immediately after the meeting, before the formal record is received. This is usually the outcome or actions from the meeting, or any decision which has been made which changes care planning for the child.

You are likely to need to update the child's chronology following attendance at a meeting or to complete a short case recording summarising the event. It is helpful to get into a habit of updating the child's chronology on a regular basis and practise summarising key information. Refer back to Chapter 1 for a reminder of the importance of chronologies and how these are constructed.

Conclusion

This chapter has considered how to record meetings in depth. We have shared the importance of practical considerations in making meetings more collaborative with families, which will hopefully reduce any anxiety, and help the social worker record what is happening more comprehensively. We have shared good practice around thoroughly planning and confidently facilitating meetings, which has a direct impact on being able to record in the meeting and to ensure accurate records are distributed afterwards. We have asked you to consider creative ways to facilitate meetings and involve families in decision making and have highlighted how SMART planning can assist with clear outcomes for children and families. These considerations can inform the agenda of meetings, again making the task of recording more straightforward overall. We ask you to consider the following questions:

What is your understanding of factors which influence good case recording in meetings?

Why is careful planning so important in influencing the case recording of meetings?

How will you use knowledge to inform how you plan, facilitate and record meetings?

Talking it Through

It is always important to extend your learning and talking things through with others can be helpful. At the end of each chapter we include a link to a video showing some students and / or practitioners talking through the content and their learning. In this video Siobhan and Rebecca meet with Camilla, an independent reviewing officer. As a previous Case Conference Chair, Rebecca has a great deal of experience in chairing meetings and so Camilla and Rebeca talk about the challenges of both chairing and recording meetings. The video discussion opens out into advice for good practice in meetings.

Chapter

7

Case Recording for Care Experienced Children and Young People

Working with children and young people who are care experienced is a vast subject area, with many excellent organisations and individual authors championing good practice, alongside children and families. In relation to case recording, good practice emphasised throughout this text, does apply to children and young people who are care experienced. However, we wish to emphasise the significance of good case recording in this area, as there are some differences and specific considerations to highlight. Personal information is viewed in legislation as 'data', but it is much, much more than this: *"Records about someone's life are key to them understanding life narrative, creating integrity of experience, building self-esteem and can also have the power to create new meanings for life events"* (Who Cares? Scotland, 2019: 3).

Who are care experienced children and young people?

There are a range of words or phrases which you may have heard historically or more recently, in this area of work, such as 'Looked After Child (LAC), 'Child Looked After (CLA)', 'foster child' and / or 'care leaver'. The Government report that there were 80,850 children looked after in England, which was up 1% on 2020 (Gov.uk, 2021). Children and young people are formally defined as 'looked after' by a local authority, under the Children Act 1989, when they are:

- *"Subject to Care Orders or Interim Care Orders (under section 31 and 38 of the Children Act 1989), who could be placed in a range of settings, including kinship placements, foster care, residential care or at home with parents*

- *Placed, or authorised to be placed, with adopters by a local authority (under section 18 (3) of the Adoption Act 2002)*
- *Voluntarily accommodated under section 20 of the Children Act 1989, including unaccompanied asylum-seeking children and young people*
- *Subject to Court Orders with residence requirements, such as secure remand or remand to local authority accommodation (section 21 of the Children Act 1989)."*

(Department of Education, 2010)

As we have already explored, the language we use has a profound effect on building relationships with children and young people, and can directly impact on the child's own identity, self-esteem and self-worth. Language also evolves and changes over time responding to research and good practice. As Brid Featherstone highlights language has the power to *"reach out, exclude, convey affection, harm, humiliate, shame and hurt"* (Social Work Action Group, 2021).

From listening to and valuing the views of children and young people, we have chosen to use the broader term of 'care experienced' child or young person throughout this chapter. The Independent Care Review Scotland heard from children and young people that 'care experience' has meaning for many: *"it has supported movement-building and is helpful as an understanding of personal identity"* (The Independent Care Review Scotland, 2020: 10). In our definition, 'care experienced' refers to anyone at any stage of their life, who has been or is currently placed in care, no matter how short the period of time. Care could mean a variety of settings, including residential care, foster care, kinship care or 'looked after' at home with parents. This term also includes children or young people who have been adopted, but were previously looked after (Who Cares? Scotland, 2021). We are mindful some children and young people do not like the word 'care' as this can have a wide range of connotations (TACT, 2019: 5), and may not be the term that children, young people and families you work with like or connect with. We would always encourage speaking directly to children, young people and families about the terms of reference they feel most comfortable with and always use their names where possible in case recording.

Pause for Reflection

The Social Work Action Group (2021) have created a brilliant video resource showcasing the power of language in social work, with contributions by parents, adults who are care experienced, academics and social work professionals. Some excerpts from this resource championing the need to consider language every single day follow. This is vital for working with all children, young people and families, but especially for those who are care experienced. You can watch the full video by following this QR code:

The statements in this video are really helpful to think about in some depth:

"Language is the foundation of communication and communication is the building block of relationships...when you reduce people to acronyms, you take away their individuality and their purpose. You reduce people to a shell of who they really are and take away they humanity and their dignity."

Taliah (Care Experienced Parent Advocate)

"Language is always changing and can be quite personal. It's really important for social workers to understand the changing nature of language, and also to ask people preferred terms, preferred language....if someone uses a word or phrase I don't like, it stops the relationship right there and then."

Vikki Walton (Social Worker and Social Work Action Group's disability representative)

"How important is language and terminology in the care sector? It's very important you know. We have to be very cautious and careful about the lexicon we use, especially because it segregates young people, it makes them feel unwanted, it makes them feel inadequate and makes them feel like robots and they're not. I felt worthless in a professional environment when I was referred to as a looked after child....we've got to somehow modernise the way we use language."

Chris Wild (Author and Campaigner for young people in care)

"It means a lot to be clear and transparent, and the words we are using mean the same things as each other. Words are the only way we can communicate by writing, so emails, reports, things like that....so that language has to be really correct, and the words used have to be representational of what everyone involved thinks. It's important to me the right words, agreed words, chosen words are used when talking about me and my family."

Nicki Lancaster (mother and art therapist)

Reflect on the terminology, phrases and terms of reference you have used in your own written case recording or in case recording you have read. Try to be as objective and constructively critical as possible and consider these reflective questions:

What alternative words or phrases could have been used instead?

Why is it so important to use language that is compassionate, inclusive, open and kind?

How can you work with colleagues to consider the use of language collectively, and how this could be changed and adapted in your organisation (perhaps in a team meeting or reflective space)?

What are the additional responsibilities for social workers working with care experienced children and young people?

The local authority, sometimes referred to as 'the corporate parent', has a unique responsibility to the children placed in their care, and those who leave their care (Department of Education, 2018: 6). In relation to all decision making, the local authority must consider the critical question *"would this be good enough for my child?"* (Department of Education, 2018: 6). Corporate parenting principles are set out in the Children and Social Work Act 2017 and include:

"Acting in the child's best interests; encouraging and taking into account the child's views, wishes and feelings; helping the child to access and make best use of services; promote high aspirations and outcomes; for children to be safe and stable in their live; and to prepare the young person for adulthood and independent living."

(Department of Education, 2018)

In practice, there are additional tasks and case recording activities for care experienced children and young people to demonstrate that these parenting principles are being achieved.

Care planning is a core element of the assessment, planning, intervention and review process which underpins social work with care experienced children, young people and their families. This is:

- *"to ensure that children and their families and the child's carers are treated with openness and honesty and understand the decisions that are made;*
- *to provide clarity about the allocation of responsibilities and tasks, in the context of shared parenting between parents, the child's carers and the corporate parents and ensure that actions lead to improved outcomes; and*
- *to demonstrate accountability in the way in which the functions of local authorities under the 1989 Act are exercised."*

(Department of Education, 2015: 22)

A huge amount of information is gathered, stored and shared throughout a child's journey, often as part of local authority processes. This often says more about administrative aspects and expectations than about experiences, relationships and outcomes for the child: *"in many ways, this information is their story, but they do not own it"* (Independent Care Review Scotland, 2020).

A care experienced child or young person will have an overarching care plan, and the circumstances that lead to a child becoming looked after will vary greatly. The overall care plan should be tailored to meet the needs of the child and provide *"a sense of permanence, be built around relationships, involve birth families and incorporate the child's perspective"* (Research in Practice, 2014: 1). There are other plans, such as the child's personal education plan (PEP), health plan and placement plan, which will contribute to the overall assessment of the child and family's needs and be presented for the child's review meetings, too. When a young person is leaving local authority care, a pathway plan is also necessary to ensure this transition is planned and successful. There may be additional care plans required for Court in the event care proceedings are initiated.

Care plans are completed within stringent timescales, prior to the child entering care or if this is not possible within 10 working days of this date, and are kept under constant review and changed as required (Department for Education, 2010). It should be possible for someone to read a care plan and gain an outline picture of the child or young person's story which is tailored to them as an individual (Research in Practice, 2014).

In addition, an Independent Reviewing Officer (IRO) be will allocated to the child or young person to offer the crucial role of ensuring the local authority completes its responsibilities as 'corporate parent', and this professional oversees, quality assures and scrutinises the care plan. The information you provide will have a direct impact on the IRO's ability to fulfil their role, so always ensure information recorded is factual, accurate and timely. Care plans may be accessed by managers with a role in overseeing your work and supervising you. They need to be able to understand where the plan is at, and what needs to happen next, too.

Focus on Practice

Research in Practice (2014) offers some really useful questions to consider when writing a care plan for children and young people, to ensure this is tailored to the child's needs and is personal and unique to them.

A sense of permanence: How have adverse circumstances undermined the child's sense of self and what will be done to rebuild this for the child?

The importance of relationships: How has the child been affected by past relationships? What steps will be taken to preserve and sustain positive relationships or to replace or improve less positive ones so that the child can be assured of good quality relationships that will endure into adulthood?

Involving birth families: How are parental problems that led to the child becoming looked after being addressed? How is the child's connection to their birth family – parents, siblings and other family members – being nurtured and preserved?

The child's perspective: Who is having ongoing conversations with the child to ascertain their wishes and feelings? How is the meaning of the child's behaviour being understood? Who is trying to imagine how the world looks from the child's perspective?'

(Research in Practice, 2014: 2)

Consider a care plan you have written for a care experienced child or young person, or one you have read:

What information would you seek and where would the information come from?

Why are the words or phrases you use to write the care plan important?

How could you use these questions to improve the quality of the care plan?

Family time

One of the key principles of the Children Act 1989 is the presumption that there should be continued family time between the child and their family while the child is in the care of the local authority. The underlying philosophy of the Act is to work in partnership with family and towards reunification where possible (Department of Education, 2015). Family time should be a primary focus shaped around the child or young person's needs, with their welfare being of paramount consideration. The child's wishes and feelings will be fully considered and assessed to ensure relationships are valued, with family members, previous carers, friends and other important people in the child or young person's life. Case recording family time is complex task, and often one which is underestimated.

The importance of language is further emphasised here in relation to care experienced children and young people having 'family time' with their loved ones. We have deliberately chosen this term 'family time', rather than 'contact' to recognise the views of care experienced children and young people. This, again, may not be the preferred term for the child or young person you are working with, and we would again reiterate and advocate asking the families directly what term they would prefer. For example, young people have stated they like alternative phrases, such as "*making plans to see our family*'; *'family meet up time'*; *'seeing Dad / Mum / Grandma'*; *'meeting with friends and family*" (TACT, 2019: 6) . For one young person it was described as "*golden time, because seeing your family is golden and it's the best time*" (TACT, 2019: 6). Let the child or young person decide and help them shape their plans! Always remember family time can include non-direct contact with family and friends, such as letters, cards, video calls, phone calls, emails and text messages. Get to know how the child or young person likes to communicate and find creative and personalised ways to meet their needs, and the needs of their loved ones.

In relation to case recording, a family time plan or agreement is always useful, and often necessary, as part of your organisation's processes. This sets out the basis and expectations of family time for all attendees, as well as any professional who may facilitate or supervise face-to-face sessions. This will always be reviewed, amended and revised on a regular basis to ensure the needs of the child and their family are met, and this is a positive experience. Remember the language you use in the agreement or plan can help build and maintain relationships, so consider words and phrases that are inclusionary, positive and child centred. The child and their family could be encouraged and supported to write this document themselves, in their own words. For younger children, a child friendly version of this document, with visual pictures or a timeline, may help them understand how and when they will be seeing or hearing from their loved ones, and what to expect.

There is sometimes the assumption made that face-to-face family time needs to be fully supervised by a professional. However, this is very much based on your risk assessment for the child and the circumstances of the family, with the risk assessment being another written document required as part of your family time plan or agreement. Family time may need to be supervised in the early days of a child becoming looked after, but perhaps not necessarily in the medium to long term, or this may be required for a specific reason. There may be circumstances where the child's family time can be facilitated, which means supported at the start and end of the session, with help from a professional to find a suitable venue for example, but full supervision may not be required. The child and their family could spend time in private together, without a supervisor being present. A family member or friend could support arranging, facilitating or supervising family time, making the experience a little more typical for the child and their family. This is where gathering and recording the right information, your analysis and creativity can make a big difference to how successful family time can be!

What should I write down?

For fully supervised family time, which may last a couple of hours or sometimes longer, it can be challenging to decide what information to record and what information to omit. It can feel unwieldly and unnecessary for every small detail to be noted, and if family time feels ordinary or unremarkable, sometimes very little is recorded at all. To write or type notes as family time is actually happening can feel uncomfortable for the supervisor and distracting for the family, however, there is also concern detail may be lost or forgotten if family time is recorded later. In addition, family time may be challenging to observe if there are a number of children and adults all together, with lots going on. Unfortunately, there is no 'one size fits all'. This is once again where thoughtful planning, thinking about the purpose of family time and how the case recordings may be used now or in the future, helps to decide what is important to write.

Pause for Reflection

Once again planning for a family time session is important in considering what you need to record. Considering some reflective questions may help you decide as each family situation is unique. For family time case recordings which may be presented to Court or be necessary to inform an assessment, what information would be helpful?

In general:

What would a child or young person want to see recorded from their family time if they access their files in later years?

Why is the information you record helpful for children, young people and families to reflect upon and learn from?

How will you ensure the case record is fit for purpose?

It is important to record factual information, without professional opinion in the content of the family time record. Remember to include the date, time and attendees of family time, and where this took place. Your organisation is likely to have a template to adhere to, which may include sections such as commenting on the arrival / start and the ending of family time. Professional analysis and evidenced-based judgement are important and should be recorded, but this is more useful presented separately, perhaps in a paragraph at the end. Once again, the written record should give a clear and vivid picture of exactly what happened and when, thinking from the perspective of someone reading the document who is unfamiliar with this child and family. Does it make sense as a stand-alone document?

Should I just observe or can I intervene?

Social workers sometimes say they do not feel comfortable intervening in family time, for example directing a parent, sharing their observations or providing support, advice and guidance whilst family time is happening. This is usually guided by the view that family time is for parents to spend uninterrupted time with their children and demonstrate their parenting skills, and the role of the supervisor is merely to observe. However, this is a very precious time for the child and their family, in what is often a very unnatural and alien setting. If a child, young person or family member is struggling or the family needs support, encouragement and guidance, then this can be offered. Not only will the relationship develop between the supervisor and the family strengthen, but the quality of family time will be enhanced for all involved, especially for the child or young person. Support, advice and guidance can feed into your assessment work, highlight the parents' skills and what help they may need for reunification to happen. Just make sure any advice, guidance or support you give is recorded factually in the case record for the family time session and if you have intervened for a specific reason, just make clear why and what action you took.

Case recordings of family time should be used to give feedback to families. This is often most useful as soon as possible after family time, so they can recall events easily, and reflect accordingly. It would be good practice to provide the family with a copy of your written case recording once completed, so they can read, digest and reflect. You could add the child, young person or family member's comments too. Do they agree with the recording? Is there something they want adding or a specific comment on the recording from their perspective? Always remember to say what went well and build on strengths. You could comment on the parent or family member's practical skills as well as their emotional responses to the child or young person and say what you observed of their relationship with their child. Feedback will also include what you feel would strengthen the next family time session. Could the child and family plan the next session themselves, such as by bringing an activity to do together? With the right venue and equipment, perhaps the parent could make a meal to enjoy with their child? Or is there a skill the parent is keen to learn or demonstrate that could be incorporated into the next session? Families feel more confident and in control if they can make decisions, which makes family time more enjoyable for all.

What do care experienced children and young people tell us about the importance of case recording?

We have tried to draw on what care experienced people tell us about case recording throughout this book. It is vital that we recognise that case recording is about people and those people are probably those that are in the best position to help us learn about best practice in case recording. We devoted the whole of Chapter 4 to writing by care experienced social workers and that is rich with learning.

Those who are care experienced may request their social work files for a wide variety of reasons, at different stages of their lives, to make sense of their past, to satisfy curiosity or to recall personal life events (Hoyle et al., 2019). Children and young people, who are not care experienced, may be able to access information about their lives more easily from relatives, friends and those within their network, and are perhaps more likely to be able to access their personal written documents and photographs more readily.

In research reported by Coram (2015), the majority of care experienced young people shared that they wanted information to help them understand why they were in care. Some young people felt information had been kept from them as a child, due to adults' perception that it may upset them. Young people reported when they did have access to their files, there were significant gaps regarding their personal histories. Young people specifically regretted how little of their personal information was stored, such as 'photographs and family mementos' (Coram, 2015: 15). This is further highlighted in research conducted by Hoyle and colleagues (2019), in which care experienced adults said the information they wanted the most, such as personal opinion, photographs and written or printed materials, were the least likely to be preserved. One care experienced adult expressed: 'I wanted nitty-gritty. I wanted photos and bills and all the minutiae that made it real. I wanted my reports and I wanted to see my handwriting' (Pugh, 1999, in Hoyle et al., 2019: 1866).

In reflecting on case recording for care experienced children and young people, the relationship between what has happened in the past, the interpretation of this within case files, and a care experienced adult's recollection of events is not always straightforward. Omissions from the child's case file may not be accidental, but a reflection of what information is seen by professionals as important to record. Records may not be balanced or aligned with the memories of care experienced children and young people but recorded from the perspective of the social worker.

Lemn Sissay MBE, the care experienced poet, author and broadcaster, reflecting on a traumatic incident from his childhood in his poignant memoir 'My Name is Why?' Sissay states: *"All the information in the reports was first curated by my foster mother and then presented to the social worker"* (Sissay, 2020: 62). His own vivid memory of this event was not recorded accurately in case file from his own recollection. Later in his memoir he makes the following profound observation on recalling events in his own life from residential care, and the impact on a child's self-worth and identity:

"Memories in care are slippery because there's no one to recall them with as the years pass…How could it matter if no one recalls it? Given that staff don't take photographs it was impossible to take something away as a memory. This is how you feel invisible. It isn't the lack of photographs that erodes the memory. It is the underlying unkindness, which makes you feel you don't matter enough. This is how to quietly deplete the sense of self-worth deep inside a child's psyche. This is how a child becomes hidden in plain sight."

(Sissay, 2020: 108)

Pause for Reflection

It's not only significant reports and Court documents which can impact on care experienced children and young people, but day-to-day interactions and reflections. Consider the following example of a daily case recording in Lemn Sissay's case file:

8/8/1983: Mrs Street, Gregory Ave [children's home] rang. Norman bought a guitar for £30 on Saturday? The source of his money'.

Lemn reflects on this case record and rightly says this *'could have read much more favourably'* by saying:

"He showed initiative in having money through his Saturday job to buy himself a guitar' and 'it is good to see that he has saved to buy, of all things, a musical instrument."

(Sissay, 2020: 145-146)

Choose a daily case recording you have completed or one you have read:

What are your initial observations?

Why is this case recording important if it were to be viewed by an adult looking back at their case record from childhood?

How could the case recording be re-framed or reworded to be more favourable for the child or young person?

Life story work

Life story work for care experienced children and young people helps them to understand their past and their identity and to make sense of their personal histories. It is essential work, with a primary goal of helping the child hold a more balanced and coherent view of their life (Wrench and Naylor, 2013). We have deliberately chosen not to go into detail about life story work in this text, as there are excellent publications on this subject which offer comprehensive information regarding attachment, trauma, loss and separation, and practical and creative ways to engage children and young people in this work. However, we wish to highlight that the quality of the information recorded in the child's case file, will inevitably have a direct impact on the quality of the life story work for a child.

Accessing social work files

The organisation 'Who Cares? Scotland' advocates for developing a "*compassionate future proof approach*" to compiling records, recognising case records should present "*a coherent narrative and should include personal / family photographs, school report cards, certificates and records of achievement and other appropriate objects and documents*" (Who Cares? Scotland, 2019: 8). However, a shift towards digital recording and scanning of non-digital records may exacerbate the loss of physical artefacts such as photographs and further fragment a care experienced person's lived experience (Hoyle et al., 2019). The statutory retention requirement for case records regarding children and young people who have been looked after by a local authority is 75 years from the date they were captured (Children Act 1989). The full impact of advances in digital recording are not yet known, such as migration of information from system to system, potentially affecting the information rights of care experienced children, young people and adults throughout this century (Hoyle et al., 2019).

Young people have shared that accessing their case records can be problematic, with little support in obtaining their information, and little emotional and psychological support once files are retrieved. Files can also be heavily redacted, due to confidentiality of a third party, meaning it can be really hard to make sense of some information.

Pause for Reflection

Care experienced adults have shared their views on accessing files from childhood in *'Our lives, our stories, our records: A record access campaign'* by Who Cares? Scotland (2019).

This document gives poignant and personal accounts from those who have accessed their social work files and is available through this QR code.

These are some of those views:

David: *"Upon receipt of my records, even though I had taken considerable time to decide I wanted to access them, I found myself to be extremely overwhelmed, upon reflection I was almost paralysed with anxiety about what might be inside the envelope."*
(Who Cares? Scotland, 2019: 9)

Lee: *"Even the process of reading my papers was done in a way to suit others and not about my need for respect and dignity and choice as to how I would like to deal with it all."*
(Who Cares? Scotland, 2019: 9)

Alice: *"There are hundreds of pages that look like this. I understand that this was to protect my mother and her right to confidentiality, but these are chunks of my life that are missing and that I'll never be able to get back."*
(Who Cares? Scotland, 2019: 6).

What are your thoughts and feelings about these accounts?

Why are these views so important for case recording?

How will these views influence your case recording now? How might that impact on care experienced adults who may read their records years down the line?

Conclusion

There are a number of additional considerations for children and young people who are care experienced. They may wish to access their records many years down the line and this has implications for what and how we write now. Care experienced people have shared their views on recording and how case records have impacted upon them as adults, which guides our practice. Once again, we have considered the language we use in case recording and highlighted good practice for making sure records are clear and accessible, and strengths-based. Finally, we ask you to think about:

What you have learned from this chapter?

Why is case recording especially important for those who are care experienced?

How will the learning from this chapter inform what you do in practice?

Talking it Through

It is always important to extend your learning and talking things through with others can be helpful. At the end of each chapter we include a link to a video showing some students and / or practitioners talking through the content and their learning. In this video Siobhan and Rebecca meet with Mary and Camilla again. Mary is a care experienced social worker who joined us to discuss her contribution to chapter 4. Camilla is an independent reviewing officer who joined us in the last chapter. We are also joined by Noel who is a social worker in a children in care team.

Chapter

8

Analysis in Case Recording

We have referred to analysis a number of times in this book – in fact the word analysis appears 38 times in the text before you get to this chapter. Case recording very much supports analysis and analysis is a key aspect of case recording, so the links are extensive. We know this can be an area which social workers are keen to develop and therefore felt a specific chapter would be useful.

The word analysis comes from the Ancient Greek word análusis which taken literally means 'a breaking up' it is therefore often viewed as being about breaking down information to look at it in more detail. Dictionary definitions of analysis generally build on this idea. For example, the Oxford Dictionary definition of analysis is *"detailed examination of the elements or structure of something to improve understanding."* Serious case reviews such as those covered in Chapter 9 and investigations which consider a lack of analysis often use the analogy of puzzle pieces (see for example, page 148), identifying that pieces of the puzzle are often missing. In some ways analysis is about breaking down information into pieces in order to make sure that all the pieces of the puzzle are available. In social work analysis is often taken forward into synthesis. The Oxford Dictionary definition of synthesis is *"the combination of components or elements to form a connected whole."* Synthesis is about putting the pieces of the puzzle together to form a fuller picture.

When we talk about analysis in social work, we generally use the word to mean a combination of analysis and synthesis, because in practice analysis goes beyond simply breaking down and presenting information to exploring what this information means and how it can be used. Essentially good social work is about understanding the whole in light of the parts. This holistic understanding only comes about through professional analysis where the parts are looked at separately and then connected so that the whole can be viewed from an informed perspective.

Reflection and analysis

In social work, analysis is often linked with reflection and there are many connections. The stages of reflection, for example, are closely aligned with analysis. Perhaps the most well-known writing about reflective practice comes from Donald Schön whose 1983 book 'The Reflective Practitioner' is generally seen as a key text. In this book, Schön proposed two very different (but potentially linked) forms of reflection:

- Reflection *in* action: this is the reflecting we do in the midst of something. The inner narrative that we have whilst undertaking a task, for example.

- Reflection *on* action: This is separate to, but linked with, reflection in action. It is the reflection done later, after the event – talking things through informally, or formally with colleagues, discussing things in supervision or reflective exploration in writing. It is in making the distinction between thinking 'on the job' and this later reflection that Schön's work has been so significant.

Almost ten years later Killion and Todnem (1991) added a third stage of reflection. They used the same phrasing that Schön had done as this had been so popular, but they claimed that Schön had missed a key stage:

- Reflection *for* action: This is the reflection done before a piece of work. This is the reflection we do in planning and thinking ahead.

In this book we have tried to encourage you to think about how all three stages of reflection are important in case recording – particularly supporting you to think about planning and preparation bearing in mind how this might impact on your case recording.

In relation to analysis most people make the links with reflection on action. However, it is important for you to be conscious of the ways in which you are making sense of information before an event, as well as how you are interpreting information during the event– this will help you to analyse all of the information as you reflect back on action.

What about *critical* analysis?

Students are often asked to complete a critical analysis on their practice and so in social work we often see critical analysis as something linked to study. However, critical analysis is a key aspect of case recording, particularly when working with complexity and considering risk.

Whenever we use the word critical in social work it is about creating connections with critical theory, bringing in an understanding of power and the socio-political context. Critical analysis therefore goes further than simple analysis, bringing in a consideration of where the information has come from and why you have been given this information. It also involves a consideration of the information in the wider context.

Wicked problems and complexity in social work

In 1973, Rittel and Webber referred to 'wicked problems' in social work, which could be characterised as:

- Having no definitive formulation
- Relating to multiple issues
- Being significantly conflictual – with conflicts of interest, conflicts of opinion and conflicts of values
- Lacking clarity about the end point goal
- Being uniquely configured, such that 'solutions' which worked in other situations may not be helpful.

(adapted from Hood et al., 2016)

Much of what we deal with in contemporary social work could be described as 'wicked problems.' The systems that we operate within and the socio-political context of our practice has become more and more complex over time. Our response to this can often exaggerate the complexity of the situation as we follow complex procedures. Good social work finds the simplicity in the complexity (Maclean, 2019). The real simplicity is that the child's needs and welfare are always paramount. The child must always be at the very centre of case recording.

The practice and product of analysis

Analysis is something that social workers *do*. It is essentially the way in which we think in practice – thereby connecting our thinking with our doing. Wilkins and Boahen (2013:11) explain that a social worker needs to develop an analytical mindset:

"By an analytical mindset, we mean an approach to practice that is repeatedly questioning the information you have, asking what information might be missing and why it might be important, actively hypothesising and considering different interpretations of the same information (without speculating too widely or too wildly). In other words, an analytical mindset is about taking an overall approach to practice and as such, it affects how one writes assessments, interacts with service users and colleagues but especially how one thinks."

However, analysis is often seen as a product rather than practice. For example it is not unusual to hear a social worker say, "I just need to do the analysis now," generally they are referring to a section of a form which they need to complete.

Lillis and Vallely (2021) explain that:

"Analysis is of course also a product, a written record which captures key aspects of all the different parts of the analytic process – the thinking, listening and observing that social workers do. The written record of analysis involves selecting the most important details from all these aspects and writing in a way that makes these understandable to many different kinds of readers. Moving from analysis as process – a part of almost every moment of everyday practice and involving a wide range of professional skills, intuition and expertise – to analysis as a written product is central to the securing of services and providing good care for vulnerable young people and adults."

The remainder of this chapter provides some hints and practical ideas for social workers in undertaking analysis and making decisions. These hints and tips should help in terms of both the practice of analysis and the product, linking this to the importance of our case recording.

Anchor principles

Brown, Moore and Turney (2012) report on a Research in Practice Development Group, which developed a set of principles to support social workers to create more analytical assessments. These principles, referred to as 'anchor principles', can support social workers to think beyond the simple presentation of information to develop an analytical understanding of the information. The principles guide a practitioner through the following five questions:

1. What is the assessment for?
2. What is the story?
3. What does the story mean?
4. What needs to happen?
5. How will we know we are making progress?

These anchoring questions can help a social worker to break down the social work process into component parts, so enabling a more analytical approach. You might be able to use these anchoring questions to help you in analysing the information you gather. Essentially the anchoring questions are about you thinking through the meaning of information you have gathered and recorded and looking towards the future.

Decision trees

Decision trees can be useful in analysing information and reaching decisions, especially in complex situations (Hood 2018, Maclean 2019). Decision trees are a specific tool used to support decision making, generally based on mathematical algorithms, they are widely used in science and industry. Decision trees are very mathematical in design, usually drawing on a range of graphs and calculations to support decision making. Increasingly, algorithms and decision trees are being trialled across social work with children and families in a range of different ways (McIntyre and Pegg, 2018) with a number of local authorities using algorithmic profiling to make initial identifications of children at risk. Analytics are widely used in contemporary society and the use of such systems is likely to increase. Social workers need to be clear about how they use a more individualised nuanced decision-making model, whilst drawing on what data is able to offer. Maclean (2019) developed a decision-making tree specific to social work, based around the spelling of the word tree, drawing on the main branches of reaching a decision in social work, as theory, research, evidence and expertise. The first letter of each word spells TREE.

Theory

Theory is vitally important in social work but its use in practice is not always well understood by practitioners. Certainly, there is a distinct lack of clarity between theories, models, methods and approaches in the social work community (Maclean, Finch and Tedam, 2018). Very often they are all lumped together in teaching, or in the literature, under the heading social work theory. In some ways whether something is a theory, a model, a method or an approach is merely semantics, but actually, understanding the differences can be really helpful in aiding social workers to be more theory-informed in their practice.

- A *theory* guides understanding and can help us to clarify what is happening in a situation (example: attachment).
- A *model* helps us to intervene in a situation (example: signs of safety) whilst a *method* is a specific tool or technique used in that intervention (example: three houses). In fact, this chapter provides some models for analysis outlining some of the methods that might be used as part of these.
- An *approach* is our overall way of going about something (example: strengths-based approach).

Therefore, in thinking about analysis we would usually draw on theories as these can help aid our understanding about a situation. In developing a suggested plan of intervention then we would generally refer to models and methods.

Research

Research evidence can be particularly helpful in considering risk indicators; likely outcomes in situations; what works in practice and the likelihood of successful change. However, it is important to take a critical, questioning approach to research. Where is the research from? What methods were used? What was the motive? Who funded it? Who carried it out? How near to practice is it? Each of these will have an impact on how valid and useful the research is and how relevant it might be to your analysis.

Dyke suggests some 'rules of thumb' in citing research in reports (Dyke, 2019: 105):

- *"Cite original research not second-hand references*
- *Only quote research that you have read and understand*
- *Never vaguely refer to 'research says...' It is important to give the full reference of the research*
- *Be honest and acknowledge if the research is ambiguous or doesn't support your argument*
- *Use the research dynamically, incorporating it into your argument."*

Pause for Reflection

Spend some time reflecting on your use of theory and research, with specific reference to case recording. The following questions might help as a prompt:

What are the general expectations in your organisation around the use of theory and research in case recording?

How do you refer to theory in your case recording?

Where do you access research?

When have you made effective use of research and / or theory?

How was it helpful?

How might you make better use of theory and research in your case recording?

Evidence

Sometimes practitioners think of 'evidence' as the information they draw from research findings. However, drawing on thinking about the whole TREE – research and evidence are separate branches. So, whilst research findings are very important in terms of social work decision making, evidence is really about a specific situation: What is known? How do you know it?

When analysing evidence then it needs to be triangulated. Triangulation has a range of different meanings in different contexts. In research, triangulation is about validating data by cross referencing the data from more than two sources (hence the triangle). According to Carvalho and White (1997) triangulation goes further than validation in that it:

- Offers a deepening and widening of understanding, especially in complex situations
- Produces innovation by providing a range of interpretations
- Enriches evidence
- Prevents the potential for bias
- Can confirm, refute or explain evidence

In social work the triangle of evidence is generally acknowledged as:

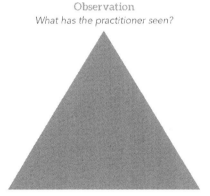

Observation
What has the practitioner seen?

Feedback
What conversations has the social worker had? What are others saying about the situation?

Product evidence
In social work, product evidence would largely be seen as documentation. So, this corner of the triangle would be about drawing on records, chronologies etc.

Good social work practice connects the evidence drawn from each corner of the triangle and the analysis, then considers the interconnectivity. For example, what is observed may contradict the feedback you have received, or the product evidence might suggest one thing whilst feedback evidence indicates something else. Digging deeper and exploring each corner of the triangle really helps with analysis.

Expertise

Fook, Ryan and Hawkins identified that:

"the study of expertise and expert practice is highly controversial... professions can be criticised for dominance over and disempowerment of the constituency they are ostensibly servicing."
(Foo, Ryan and Hawkins., 2000: 4)

The very notion of expertise can be disempowering. Who is the expert? Why are they an expert? The expertise branch of the decision tree recognises this and draws on expertise in a partnership-based manner. Increasingly, in practice, there is a recognition that people can become experts through experience and not simply through training and study. In social work there has long been a view that service users are the experts about their own situations. There is a widening recognition that people with lived experiences of systems can add a great deal to the evidence base we draw on, so the voice of the care experienced community is increasingly being listened to.

In many ways each stakeholder in any situation has expertise in their position. So, for example a social worker may have some expertise in the systems that support families, a health visitor may hold expertise about child development, health and wellbeing, a teacher may have expertise in the educational context, the family has expertise about their circumstances, and children have expertise about their experiences. So, drawing on expertise as part of the decision tree calls for the practitioner to consult widely with all those who hold expertise in the situation. It also calls for the practitioner to draw on their own experience or practice wisdom. Perhaps most importantly it requires the social worker to be attuned to the power dynamics – who is the 'expert' and why?

An argument could be made that rather than expertise, the final branch of the decision tree should be experience. However, it is important to recognise that each person's experiences may be very different and how each person understands their experiences will differ. Herein lies expertise, each person with experience (whether that be professional experience or lived experience) can only be an expert on their own situation. The individual expertise in any given situation must be considered as just that – individual and unique to any given situation.

Professional expertise is about drawing on each branch of the decision tree – theory, research, evidence and a range of expertise and then connecting each branch to be clear about the 'reach' of the tree.

Pause for Reflection

Think about a family that you are working with (or maybe a case study you have been given if you are a student). Reflect on the following questions:

Who is involved in this family's life?

What expertise does each person hold?

What expertise have you drawn on in your work with this family?

Why this expertise?

How has this impacted on your work with this family?

Models and methods for analysis and decision making

There are many models which can be used to aid reflection, analysis and decision making. They can be used to consider the information you have gathered and recorded in the child's file. They will help you make sense of the information, reflect, analyse, make decisions and plan. A range of methods, or tools, can be drawn out of these models. Some of the models and methods we think you might find useful are covered on the following pages. Developing your social work practice is about trying new tools and sharing your learning with colleagues. Don't forget that different models and methods will be useful in different circumstances.

 **SHARE**

SHARE (Maclean, Finch and Tedam, 2018) can be used in a wide range of ways but is essentially a model of analysis. SHARE spells out five separate, but interconnected components which are important in social work practice. Seeing, Hearing, Action, Reading and Evaluation. As such it encourages a social worker to consider what they have seen in a situation, what they have heard, what actions they (and others) have taken and what they have read before evaluating all of this information. SHARE therefore adopts a triangulated approach.

SHARE recognises that two people can have a completely different view of a situation, because they have a different SHARE. So, two social workers might visit the same family and come away with a different view about what is going on and what needs to happen. This might be because they have seen something different, or heard things differently, or maybe one social worker has read something that the other hasn't.

A key aspect of SHARE, which makes it different from other models, is that it encourages a consideration of the person's experiences. For example, when considering SHARE in assessment, the model suggests taking account of:

SHARE		SOCIAL WORKER	CHILD
Seeing	👁	What have you seen? (Drawing on observational skills)	How do they view you, the social worker? What do they see? How do you know?
Hearing	👂	What have you heard? Who from?	What do they hear from their family? What do they hear from you - what kind of language do you use?
Action	✋	What have you done? What impact has that had?	What do their actions tell you?
Reading	📖	What have you read? (previous case notes, research, legislation, theory, etc)	If they read what is written about them, how would it leave them feeling?
Evaluation	☁	How are you evaluating the situation?	How do they evaluate the social work intervention or how will they in the future?

What? Why? How?

We have used the What? Why? How? framework as a basis throughout this text. In fact, this is a useful framework to consider when thinking about analysis in case recording. Analytical recording is clear about:

- What is happening
- Why this situation has come about
- How it is impacting on the child or young person

Dyke asserts that analysis should *"address causation and implication, as well as just information."* (Dyke, 2019:104) In the What? Why? How? framework:

- What is about the information
- Why is about the causation
- How is about the implication

Case recording generally provides lots of information, describing what happened but may give little about why and how. This can be because social workers are concerned about moving away from fact. However, analysis must contain answers to the key 'why?' and 'how?' questions. It is in understanding and analysing the why and the how that professional expertise is utilised. Unless we understand why something might be happening and how it is impacting on people it is difficult to develop a clear plan about what should happen. All the questions of the framework are therefore connected in the analysis that we do as social workers.

Simon Sinek presents the idea of the golden circle and suggests that it is always the most effective to 'start with why' (2019.) Essentially, the why question is the starting point for analysis in social work. This is illustrated by Rogers and Allen (2019: 121) who suggest using the same three questions of the what? why? how? framework but they start with why, asserting that *"an analysis asks 'why is this happening?', 'what is the impact?', 'how is this significant?'"*

It is important to recognise that the focus on the why question is about the professional expertise process. We would suggest using 'why?' very sparingly in conversation with families. Be aware that when we ask 'why?' of families it can come across as judgmental or accusative. Restorative question methods avoid asking people 'why?' because of the difficulties that can be created. With the focus on the why question in this book and particularly this chapter we think it is vitial to reinforce the importance of a careful use of the why question when we are gathering information from people. Don't avoid the question altogether but do be aware of the potential impact.

 ## What? So what? and now what?

Borton (1970) developed a model of reflection for education based around these three key questions. Borton's book 'Reach, Touch and Teach' is seen as a key text in promoting a humanist approach to learning and the model is based on an experiential learning approach. It was designed to support pupils in learning about writing in more depth and can therefore be useful in considering analysis in record keeping. Borton's original model has been further developed by Driscoll (2000) and Rolfe et al. (2001). It is often used as a model of reflection by supervisors to enable a practitioner to move from description and 'story telling' towards analysis and planning for future action. The following questions from the framework for reflection:

What? What has happened? This helps to set the scene for the subsequent questions:

So what? What is the importance, relevance or impact of what has happened?

Now what? What should happen now? It is important that in addressing this question it is clear why this future action is being suggested. Rogers asserts *"when proposing recommendations, you should not just describe what should happen next, but provide evidence or explain why something is appropriate and will work best"* (Rogers, 2020: 202). This is where expertise and analysis come together.

The information you have recorded in the child's file can be analysed using this model. What does the information tell us? What does it mean for this child and family? What will we do next?

 First, Worst, Last

Some models have specific analytical tools which need to be used if you are working within that model. Tools can always be used outside of the model, too. So, for example, you might find some analysis tools drawn out of particular models useful. Signs of Safety (Turnell and Edwards, 1999) draws on a helpful tool of considering the 'first, worst and last' of a behaviour or incident. This can be helpful in analysis to explore the frequency and severity of a behaviour which can assist particularly when exploring risk.

Pause for Reflection

Which of the methods suggested so far do you want to try in practice?

What draws you to these methods?

How will you use them in your case recording?

Thinking about the SCOPE of information

A SWOT analysis is a tool used across a range of disciplines in order to analyse information. Often used in the development of business plans the SWOT tool is particularly helpful in planning. SWOT stands for Strengths, Weaknesses, Opportunities and Threats. The idea is that in considering these four areas the analysis will be balanced. The tool has been adapted in a range of ways, for example as a learning tool, SLOT (Strengths, Learning needs, Opportunities and Threats). Dalzell and Sawyer (2011) suggest that a SCOR analysis can be helpful in social work specifically (Strengths, Challenges, Opportunities, Risks).

Starting from a SWOT analysis and looking at different iterations of it, we have developed the SCOPE tool. The dictionary definition of scope is "*the extent of the area or subject matter that something deals with or to which it is relevant*". As we have covered, analysis is essentially about breaking down information and thinking about relevance and meaning. Therefore, thinking about the scope of information in developing an analysis, particularly a critical analysis, can be helpful. To consider the SCOPE of information think about:

Strengths: Throughout this text we have encouraged a strengths-based approach to case recording. There are always strengths in any situation. An analysis should start with these.

Challenges: This should consider challenges from every angle. What challenges do the family face? Perhaps what challenges are faced by services in supporting the family?

Opportunities: What are the opportunities in this situation and how can we use these to build on the identified strengths?

Problems: What is the presenting problem with this family? What other problems do the family face? What risks are there? In what ways might this be a 'wicked problem'?

Evaluation: Evaluation is generally against a standard. In working through the SCOPE of information there may be some standards or criteria that the information can be evaluated against. For example, is there a potentially relevent risk checklist or are there research findings that could be used to evaluate the information?

Final advice

Don't avoid 'I'

The analysis of information will usually include the first-person voice (for example, "I have therefore concluded…"). Social workers can feel uncomfortable with this and may avoid the use of the first person or active voice preferring instead to use a passive voice (for example, "It has been suggested that…") There is a significant danger here that information is lost or becomes confused. Ownership of professional judgment or action is vital. The following quote from a youth offending team manager illustrates this clearly:

"As part of my work I read a large number of records and reports. In Youth Offending, AssetPlus is the assessment and planning tool which we use. This is designed to recognise the professional judgement of practitioners in order to promote more sharply focused intervention plans for children and young people. A number of the practitioners on my team (who come from a range of backgrounds) seem to struggle with making the AssetPlus more than a descriptive account. They sometimes seem fearful of 'getting things wrong'. I recognise that there is a perception about a blame culture but what I (and the courts) really value is the skills in analysis of a professional who is able to evidence a professional recommendation which leads into a defensible decision. The apparent fear about putting the word I into a professional document worries me greatly."

(Alton, quoted in Maclean, Finch and Tedam, 2018.)

When drawing on the first-person voice be clear about where your ideas have come from – have you drawn on theory, research, evidence and expertise? Using the first-person voice is about more than your 'gut' instinct. This is about your professional voice.

Use connective words

Connective words are words which connect sentences and paragraphs. They are particularly helpful in analysis as they can assist the writer to highlight relationships between ideas. Connectives can be used to:

- Add in new ideas: also, furthermore, in addition
- Establish cause and effect: therefore, as a result, because, since, so
- Provide contrast: whereas, though, however, conversely
- Provide comparison: similarly, like, in the same manner
- Indicate impact or results: hence, accordingly, consequently
- Show purpose: to this end, with this in mind, with the purpose of
- Summarise: in summary, in conclusion, overall.

Connective words can enable you to create a logical argument, but it is important to recognise that keeping the writing clear and articulate is important. It is obvious when someone has got a thesaurus out to try and use a wider variety of words.

Indeed, in 2015 a family court Judge was highly critical of a social worker's report, commenting that the assessment of a Grandmother for a Special Guardianship order, *"might just as well have been written in a foreign language"* (Silman, 2015). For the Judge this raised concerns about how far the social worker had been able to communicate and work effectively with the family. The Judge highlighted one particular obtuse paragraph, which read as follows:

"I do not intend to address the couple's relationship suffice it to say it is imbued with ambivalence: both having many commonalities emanating from their histories that create what could be a long-lasting connection or alternative relationship that are a reflection of this. Such is this connection they may collude to undermine the placement." (Ibid)

In trying to ensure your analysis reads professionally, do be careful that it makes sense.

Conclusion

In this chapter we have explored the nature of analysis as both a process and a product, highlighting the vital importance of analysis in effective case recording. We have suggested some particular tools which can be helpful in developing analysis in record keeping. Many of the tools, for example SHARE, SCOPE and the decision TREE are based on acrostic word compositions and therefore this chapter concludes in a similar vein. Maclean (2019: 211) suggests that using the word analysis and breaking it down as follows can be helpful in summarising what analysis in social work means:

Accuracy: It is important to ensure that all of the information you have is accurate.

New: Always be open to new information changing the picture.

Acknowledge: Acknowledge any missing or conflicting information.

Look: Look carefully at each piece of information and its interconnections with other information.

You: Be clear on how you see things. Your perspective, your role etc will change the way that you interpret information. Everyone sees things in different ways, so your sense of self is vitally important in being analytical.

Scepticism: Take a healthily sceptical approach, question the information you have. Why do I have that information? Where did it come from? This should lead you onto:

Investment: Consider who has vested interests in the way that information is interpreted and who has an investment in the decision-making process.

Synthesis: When the information has been considered in parts then it must be looked at in terms of the whole picture.

As a final reflection use the What? Why? How? framework:

What do you think analysis means? Has your definition changed as you have read this chapter?

Why is it important to include analysis in case recording?

How might you improve the analysis you include in your recording?

Talking it Through

It is always important to extend your learning and talking things through with others can be helpful. At the end of each chapter we include a link to a video showing some students and / or practitioners talking through the content and their learning. In this video, Siobhan and Rebecca are joined again by Nicola, an independent social worker, and Kelly, a newly qualified social worker in a CAMHs team. We are also joined for the first time by Cat, a social worker in a child protection team.

Chapter
9

Learning Lessons from Child Safeguarding Practice Reviews

We are all aware of high-profile child deaths, such as those of Victoria Climbié, Peter Connelly and Daniel Pelka, which over the years have hit the media. More recently the murders of Star Hobson and Arthur Labinjo-Hughes resulted in a joint national review entitled 'Child Protection in England' (The Child Safeguarding Practice Review Panel, 2022). The emotive nature of a child death to abuse or neglect can result in significant political and professional consequences. To the public and often professionals alike, it can feel unbelievable that opportunities can be missed, and children die in such tragic circumstances. It is recognised that public debate within the media often over-simplifies the issues, primarily seeking to assign blame, meaning Practice Reviews *"take place in an atmosphere that can make it difficult to be open and transparent, and to learn and create meaningful change"* (ADCS, 2015: 18). Media interest is not new, and extensive new coverage of child abuse and neglect began in the 1970s with the death of Maria Colwell. This continued over the decades with other high-profile cases such as those of Tyra Henry and Kimberly Carlile in the 1980s, and scandals in Cleveland, Rochdale and Orkney in the late 1980s and 1990s (Elsley, 2010). The Child Safeguarding Practice Review Panel (2020) succinctly stresses the complexity of child protection work:

"The problem is false positives: thousands of families have the same risk factors, but their children do not die and they are not seriously harmed. The inherent tension in child protection practice is how best to identify those children most at risk without pulling into the child protection system thousands of families who would never seriously harm their children."

(The Child Safeguarding Practice Review Panel, 2020: 6)

What is a Child Safeguarding Practice Review?

The purpose of a Child Safeguarding Practice Review (referred to as Practice Review hereafter), which replaced Serious Case Reviews (SCR) in 2019, is to identify local learning for practitioners to promote the safety and wellbeing of children. The Munro Review of Child Protection (2011) provided the foundation for this shift, with Munro stressing the need to focus on cause and analysis, as opposed to blame on an individual or organisation following a significant incident. This learning can be of national significance in understanding systemic issues, and to consider how policy and practice needs to change countrywide (HM Government, 2018). Working Together identifies Practice Reviews take place when:

- *"abuse or neglect of a child is known or suspected <u>and</u>*
- *the child has died or been seriously harmed"*

(Working Together, 2018: 85)

A rapid review is now undertaken on all serious incidents which are reported to 'The Child Safeguarding Practice Panel'. These set out the facts within 15 working days to establish whether there is immediate action needed to ensure a child's safety; the potential for practice learning; and a decision regarding the commissioning of a local practice review (Department of Education, 2019). Within this new system a thorough rapid review can form the basis of a full Practice Review, and in some cases avoid the need for a Practice Review at all. Rapid reviews are not made available to the public, but if undertaken, a Practice Review is.

It has been highlighted in the past that front line practitioners have not always read Serious Case Reviews, even though these reports include considerable information to inform practice (ADCS, 2015). Reviews were criticised for paying little attention to making final reports accessible for practitioners, and practitioners rarely contributed to the process (ACDS, 2015). The new system of Practice Reviews aspires to encourage safeguarding partners to focus on the voices of children, families and practitioners (The Child Safeguarding Practice Review Panel, 2020).

In terms of statistics, the NSPCC report in the UK there have been on average 58 child deaths per year, over the last 5 years, *"due to assault or undetermined intent"* (NSPCC, 2021: 1). As tragic as this figure is, we must remember that there are few child deaths in England, in comparison to other countries, and the system we have is considered one of the most effective in safeguarding vulnerable children in the world (Department of Education, 2019; The Safeguarding Practice Review Panel, 2020). There are many excellent social work practice examples where children and families are successfully supported, and risks are significantly reduced. These sadly do not attract the same level of public attention, and we must be careful not to heatedly overreact to extreme, emotive and heart-breaking cases, and change practices which do not reflect the core work. The majority of child protection focuses on chronic neglect. Neglect accounts for almost half of children subject to child protection plans, with the second highest category being emotional harm (National Statistics, 2021). Fatalities and serious sexual and physical harm for children, thankfully, is not the norm.

The Public Inquiry into the death of Victoria Climbié

Victoria Climbié tragically died over 20 years ago in February 2000, yet her case remains a significant one in our current learning of the importance of clear and accurate case recording. Originally from the Ivory coast and residing with Marie-Therese Kouau and Carl John Manning (great aunt and aunt's partner) in London, Victoria finally died of hyperthermia, after months of neglect and abuse at the hands of her carers, with 128 injuries all over her body (Laming, 2003). The Home Office pathologist who examined Victoria's body described this as the *"worst case of child abuse he had ever seen"* (Guardian, 2001). The Public Inquiry, led by Lord Laming, is over 400 pages long and scrutinises those individual professionals and agencies involved in the case, revealing shocking and distressing information about her short life.

There were many, many documented instances of referrals, conversations, observations, management decisions and general information which were not recorded at all. This was noted for many of the agencies involved, not just social care departments. Other recordings were deemed inadequate or were missing vital pieces of information or professional opinion. Information was not shared adequately between professionals and agencies, or between different local areas where the family presented. The Inquiry highlights systemic concerns in each local authority, such as the high turnover of staff, significant caseloads and inadequate recording systems. Staff in the local authority of Brent, for example, were described as 'overburdened' and 'overworked' (Laming, 2003: 77). In June 1999 it was noted that in this local area *"that only 107 referrals (42 per cent) were logged onto the system within one working week, and 41 (16 per cent) took between four and 12 weeks"* (Laming, 2003: 77). This caused inevitable and considerable delay for families, with the inadequacies of case recording being emphasised right from the point of referral.

There are 107 recommendations within the report for a range of agencies, including social care, healthcare and Police, and a number of these are pertinent to case recording and information sharing. One recommendation is a reminder, very relevant for today, of the necessity to check information and robustly plan what information is required on all home visits. This report states:

"Social workers must not undertake home visits without being clear about the purpose of the visit, the information to be gathered during the course of it, and the steps to be taken if no one is at home. No visits should be undertaken without the social worker concerned checking the information known about the child by other child protection agencies. All visits must be written up on the case file."

(Laming, 2003: 375)

The cumulative failure by Ealing social care to record basic information, meant Victoria's needs were never fully assessed within this local authority, and *"limited reactive and ineffective social work followed"* (Laming, 2003: 60). Case recording throughout Victoria's was described as *"grossly inadequate"*, with conversations directly with Victoria *"limited to little more than 'hello how are you?"* (Laming, 2003: 66). There was minimal assessment work, and this involved the writing down of limited and sometimes contradictory information provided by Victoria's great aunt, Kouao (Laming, 2003: 66). This Inquiry really highlights the lack of professional curiosity and lack of Victoria's voice. A key recommendation in the report is for the child to be seen and spoken to before any assessment can be approved by a manager. Additionally, in verbal evidence for the Inquiry, one senior practitioner shared her observations of Kouao, stating she appeared 'forceful' and 'manipulative' (Laming, 2003: 64). These judgements were never recorded, stressing the importance of evidence based professional opinion in our case records. Practitioners can shy aware from such detail in their case recording for fear of presenting as judgemental.

What do other high-profile cases say in relation to case recording?

Inadequate case recording within and between agencies has been a key finding in a number of Serious Case Reviews. This includes the high-profile deaths of Daniel Pelka (Lock, 2013), Peter Connelly (Department of Education, 2010), and Kyra Ishaq (Radford, 2010). In the case of Daniel Pelka, a number of agencies were highlighted as having missed key pieces of case recording, including school, GP and the Police. Basic checks were not completed, and information was shared inconsistently between agencies, and between geographical areas. Referrals were made to the children's social work service for concerns regarding Daniel, however at times the agency's responses and outcomes were not recorded, and seriously concerning information not acted upon. In summary the author of this review states:

"*Case recording, not only for Coventry City Council Children, Learning and Young People Directorate (CLYP) was frequently problematic and often not in line with procedures. Significant pieces of information were not always fully evidenced..... examples of poor record keeping were very concerning and demonstrated a failure of the most basic aspect of child protection work.*"

(Lock, 2013: 67)

One of the most high profile cases in which a national inquiry was held is that of Peter Connolly, also known as Baby P. The death of Baby P shook the nation. There was overwhelming media interest in this case with 2823 mentions of Baby P in UK newspapers over a 12 month period commencing on 1st November 2008 following convictions in Court (Elsley, 2010). Tracey Connelly (mother) pleaded guilty of causing or allowing the death of a child or vulnerable person, Tracey's partner, Steven Barker, and Barker's brother, Steven Owen were found guilty of the same offence. Peter Connelly's injuries were highlighted by the media, as well as the extensive professional contact with him during his short life, and the fact this was the same local authority where Victoria Climbié had died (Elsley, 2010). Public reactions were not restricted to the traditional newspaper format, but advances in technology means that online media "*provides a way individuals and interest groups can contribute to news stories in a more dynamic way*" (Elsley, 2010: 4). The negative media coverage of social workers had a widespread impact (Elsley, 2010).

In Peter's case, the 'rationale' for decisions "*was not consistently or clearly documented*" (Haringey Local Safeguarding Children's Board, 2008: 57). Inaccuracies were noted on child protection conference minutes and in legal documents. Only two sets of core groups minutes were evident on the recording system, and although other meetings had taken place and contemporaneous notes were made available for the actual review, this meant the core group would not have had this information available to "*guide their implementation of the child protection plan*" at the time (Haringey Local Safeguarding Children's Board, 2008: 104). In relation to wider family, school records for older siblings did not show any information regarding family relationships, and there was criticism of lack of direct work with older siblings by social workers, as the assessment focused on Peter. Basic information was not updated, such as composition of the household, to re-assess the family circumstances. There is acknowledgement that Tracey Connelly may have hid her intimate relationship with Jason Barker, however the inquiry considers this information may not have been apparent due to not being asked "*pertinent questions*" by professionals (Haringey Local Safeguarding Children's Board, 2008: 96). It is noted Tracey Connelly provided Jason Barker's name as her next of kin when attending hospital for herself, for example, so she had not completely hidden the facts from professionals. Regarding multi-agency working there were noted discrepancies and confusion in agency case records. Although it is concluded that Peter Connelly could and should have been safeguarded, the rare element of assessing a dangerous parent is recognised in this case:

"*The uncooperative, anti-social and even dangerous parent / carer is the most difficult remaining challenge for safeguarding and child protection services. The parents / carers may not immediately present as such, and may be superficially compliant, evasive, deceitful, manipulative and untruthful. Practitioners had the difficult job of identifying them among the majority of parents who are merely dysfunctional, anxious and ambivalent.*"

(Jones, 2009: 67).

Peter's case further emphasises that protecting children is an incredibly challenging task.

Kyra Ishaq died from an infection brought on by severe malnutrition in 2008. She was severely starved, with 60 injuries on her body at the time of death, from a sadistic regime which included punishment beatings, cold baths and being forced to overeat until she was sick (The Guardian, 2010). Angela Gordon (mother) and Gordon's partner, Junaid Abuhamz, were convicted of manslaughter. The Serious Case Review highlighted Abuhamz's strong belief in 'evil spirits' (Radford, 2010: 2). Kyra had also been withdrawn from school. There are some good examples of case recording in Kyra's case, especially in relation to health and education records, but again missed opportunities. In relation to home schooling, it is noted that the Education Welfare Officer *"whilst not undertaking any assessment, also did not make any record of events and reinforces the view that the home visit was both poorly planned, conducted and that a lack of child focus and professional curiosity was evident throughout"* (Radford, 2010: 95). The children were not seen or spoken to at this time, and the report identifies examples of a *"lack of appropriate child focus"* (Radford, 2010: 95).

Kyra's case highlights specific issues in relation to culture and identity. There are references to her family's ethnicity, but this is not consistent. The family's ethnicity is described as Black, with different members being recorded as Black Caribbean, Black African, or Black British (Radford, 2010). It is unclear how the family themselves would identify and where the information is obtained from, and beyond this *"little was known about the cultural environment of this family"* (Radford, 2010: 27). This is echoed in the Serious Case Review of 4-year-old Hamza Khan, who was neglected and starved over a period of months by his mother, Amanda Hutton, whose own mental health was severely impaired (Turney, 2016). Hamza was of mixed heritage (Pakistani and White British), and his Serious Case Review highlighted that the *"cultural and religious complexity of this family was not enquired into"* (Bradford Children's Safeguarding Board, 2013: 52). This lack of exploration was specifically criticised in this review given Hamza resided in Bradford, an area described as having *"a rich history and diversity of culture, religion and language"* (Bradford Children's Safeguarding Board, 2013: 52).

There is an absence of in-depth discussions regarding race, ethnicity and cultural dynamics noted in Serious Case Reviews for children of Black and mixed ethnicity backgrounds on the whole (Bernard and Harris, 2016). The importance of examining background, culture, religion and individual identity is recognised, yet the latest triennial review of Serious Case Reviews, analysed between 2014-2017, continues to identify that whilst ethnicity may be recorded, the implications for the day-to-day experiences for children are not explored which *"reflects a wider challenge for all children's cases not just those from minority, ethnic groups"* (Brandon et al, 2020: 19).

Arthur Labinjo-Hughes and Star Hobson

Devastatingly, during the writing of this book, two young children in different local authorities were murdered by their respective female step-parents. These children are Arthur Labinjo-Hughes and Star Hobson. The cases have been very prominent in the news, with the public and politicians calling for significant change to how vulnerable children are supported and risks managed (Department for Education, 2021). Following the decision to place Bradford's children's services under a new Trust, Star and Arthur's cases were joined together in a national review.

Sadly, there are some well-known and repeated concerns in relation to case recording. The review highlights limited direct work with both children, and a lack of understanding of what their life was truly like (Child Safeguarding Practice Review Panel, 2022). The report emphasises the poor use of language in case recording. For example, it states *"Star was recorded as displaying 'secure attachment' with her mother without explanation of what this meant or looked like"* (Child Safeguarding Practice Review Panel, 2022: 88). In both cases, concerns reported by their wider family members were recorded as *'malicious'* (pg. 89). In relation to information sharing, the review highlights three key issues: *"a lack of timely and appropriate information sharing; limited information seeking; and evidence not being pieced together and considered in the round"* (Child Safeguarding Practice Review Panel, 2022: 93). The review vehemently states:

"Time and again we see that different agencies hold pieces of the same puzzle but no one holds all of the pieces or is seeking to put them together."
(Child Safeguarding Practice Review Panel, 2022: 93)

What have we learned from serious case reviews involving adolescents?

As we can see, the majority of high profile individual child deaths which hit the media are often younger children. It is likely this is due to the shock factor that children so young and reliant on adults for the majority of their care needs are so badly let down. However, it is acknowledged in the literature that adolescence is a vulnerable period in childhood, alongside advancements in our understanding of the adolescent brain (Heyes and Fen Hui, 2015; Firmin, 2020; Brandon et al, 2020). There has been an increase over the years in serious case reviews involving children over the age of 11 years. Over the period 2014 and 2017, there were 115 (31%) of serious case reviews involving children agreed 11 years and over, with 65 reviews relating to death and 50 reviews involving serious harm (Brandon et all, 2020). This is almost a third of the children in the cases under review.

The way adolescents face and experience risk differs from earlier childhood, with complex risks posed not only by family, but sometimes from peers, adults outside of the family home and from partners (Firmin et al, 2019). Adolescent neglect has been recognised as a particular area of concern (Hicks and Stein, 2015; Raws, 2016). Social media use and exploitation have been identified as *"new and emerging threats"* in Working Together to Safeguard Children (HM Government, 2018: 14). The evidence in serious case reviews of multiple difficulties for adolescents is stark, with factors such as substance misuse, special educational needs, school exclusions, anti-social behaviour, criminal activity, loss and separation and involvement with children's services due to abuse and neglect featuring. The complexity for safeguarding adolescents is significant:

"Professionals working in the multi-agency safeguarding system struggle to provide an effective service to vulnerable adolescents who display a range of complex behaviours and needs leaving them with a fragmented and reactive response to different aspects of their behaviour."

(Brandon et al, 2020: 65)

Research and analysis into areas such as child sexual exploitation (CSE), child criminal exploitation (CCE) and County Lines has advanced in recent years (Department for Education, 2017; Home Office, 2018; The

Children's Society, 2021). Public inquiries and serious case reviews into CSE in geographical areas of the UK such as Rochdale (Klonowski, 2013), Rotherham (Jay, 2014) and Oxford (Bedford, 2015) and are well documented and reported heavily in the media. These scandals impacted on the lives of hundreds of children over a period of many years. Concerns relating to inadequate case recording and ineffective and bureaucratic IT systems are stressed (Klonowski, 2013; Jay, 2014). The language used by professionals was also emphasised. This includes the terminology around ethnicity, which was criticised for inaccuracy, for example *'Asian'* was often written rather than *'Pakistani'* (Bedford, 2015: 6). The attitude towards victims and how risks were framed by professionals was also significant, with language demonstrating a lack of understanding of CSE and with *"crimes against them [victims] not being recorded as such"* (Bedford, 2015: 6). Bedford also notes specific language used in case records such as the word *'boyfriend'* for children as young as 13 years in abusive relationships with boys and men in their late teens to early 30s. This word deflected from the awful abuse being experienced. He highlights the following words and phrases:

"[The missing person] is believed to be prostituting herself... to pay for drugs', 'putting themselves at risk',
'She is a streetwise girl who is wilful...'
'She associates with adults who have warnings for firearms and drugs. It is possible she is prostituting herself'
'... Deliberately puts herself as risk as she goes off with older men that are strangers" (Bedford, 2015: 39)

Ultimately this language had consequences for these children and delayed protection. Labelling acted as a barrier to intervention. In relation to terminology, it feels shocking to consider that until 2015, the term *"child prostitution"* was still used in the Sexual Offences Act 2003 (Eaton and Holmes, 2017), with the Government issuing a new definition of CSE in 2017 making clear this is a *"form of sexual abuse"* (Department of Education, 2017). Once again, this highlights that the words we use and how we frame abuse and neglect is imperative to understanding the risks faced. The language used is important for building relationships, and ultimately in safeguarding children and young people.

What are the key areas for development we have learned from Serious Case Reviews?

There are a number of key points highlighted in the literature on Serious Case Reviews, Public Inquiries and Practice Reviews. In summary:

- Basic information is vital. Updating key information on a regular basis is essential. This includes asking direct questions about family composition and new adults on the scene.

- The child's voice is paramount. It is clear in this chapter that some children have not been spoken to at all and their voices absent from records. Professionals in other cases have 'seen' the child, and sometimes on a regular basis, but have not engaged with the child or exhibited professional curiosity to truly understand the child's day-to-day experiences. The child's voice needs to be recorded and clear in their case file, at all stages of your work.

- Exploring and recording information regarding a child's cultural heritage is important. This is not just about recording the correct ethnicity, but really understanding what the day-to-day experiences are for the child.

- The importance of accurately recording ethnicity for perpetrators is further highlighted in serious case reviews relating to CSE. This is needed for accurate analysis, sharing relevant information, and comprehensive multi-agency working.

- Don't shy away from curiosity and professional judgements. Make clear in the case recording when you are expressing professional opinion and make sure you have information, such as observation to evidence your views. This tells an important story for other professionals encountering the family, especially where there is limited engagement, hostility or aggression.

- Keeping on top of case recording is a challenge, especially as a busy professional working with multiple families, however Serious Case Reviews and Practice Reviews highlight the necessity to prioritise this task. Case recording is not secondary to successfully engaging with families, but complementary to (and part of) successfully engaging with families. There are clear implications for thorough decision making and planning for all children, with the aid of up-to-date and accurate case recording.

- The knock-on effect of poor case recording has serious implications for information sharing and effective multi-agency working for all children. Good quality case recording is key to good practice.

Accessing Child Safeguarding Practice Reviews

There are numerous Serious Case Reviews and Practice Reviews completed which can be accessed, and there is learning from each. The NSPCC has an extensive repository of serious case reviews, where summaries and full reports can be accessed. Every Local Safeguarding Children's Partnership (LSCP) publishes Practice Reviews within their local area. It is helpful to explore these sources and look at Practice Reviews first-hand to consider issues raised in your local area.

 Conclusion

This chapter has highlighted some themes identified in relation to case recording and the significance of this in our daily practice, which we hope supports your understanding and encourages personal and professional scrutiny. To end, we share the views of Ron Lock commenting in Daniel Pelka's Serious Case Review:

"Professional accountability for record keeping, timely reports and recording of key actions from multi agency meetings, is central to professional childcare practice, and to fail to complete appropriate records will significantly compromise inter agency working and reduce the collective ability of agencies to protect children."

(Lock, 2013: 72)

Case recording plays a vital role in safeguarding and protecting children, so in conclusion, we ask you to consider the following questions:

What do Practice Reviews tell us about the importance of case recording?

Why is case recording important in safeguarding children and young people?

How will knowledge from Practice Reviews inform your own case recording?

 Talking it Through

It is always important to extend your learning and talking things through with others can be helpful. At the end of each chapter we include a link to a video showing some students and / or practitioners talking through the content and their learning. In this video we meet Kulchuma again. Kulchuma is a school social worker and she joined us to discuss her learning from chapter 1. We also meet David again. David is a care experienced social worker and he joined us to discuss his top tips in chapter 4. We also meet Kai for the first time. Kai is a social work student. Be aware that some of the conversation about discussing culture with families contains some words which are offensive.

Chapter
10

What Can We Do? Practical Tips for Effective Case Recording

As we have discovered in previous chapters, ensuring accurate and comprehensive case recording is not as straightforward as it appears. What we do know is that good quality case recording really helps us provide effective support and help to children and their families, and is fundamental to reflection, analysis and planning. Case recording is not a separate task to forming positive relationships with children and families, it can absolutely contribute to forming positive relationships with children and families. It makes a difference, and is a fundamental part of social work. As social workers, we are hugely privileged in being privy to personal and sensitive information, often at critical and challenging times in people's lives. We have a responsibility to do our very best to record the information of children, young people and families well, and for this information to help us provide the best help and support for them. Drawing together information from previous chapters, we will highlight our top tips for case recording, and how, as social workers, we can strive to achieve these every day in this final chapter.

Get the basic information right

There is no surer way to upset or alienate a child, young person or their family members than getting their personal information wrong. This could be a simple error through inaccurately recording the spelling of a name or date of birth, or more serious mistakes. Of course, simple errors can and do happen. We are only human. However, even simple mistakes can make families feel disrespected and unimportant from the start of your intervention, impacting on their trust in you as a professional and your working relationship with them going forwards. Getting accurate information can be tricky if there are communication difficulties, a learning or mental health need, or language barrier for a child, young person or their family members.

What can we do?

From your first involvement with a family, check all the basic details are correct. Families value social workers who take time to listen and who want to get it right, so even if a family has had lots of previous social work intervention, double check name spellings, dates of birth, household members, other professionals involved and up-to-date contact information. You can make notes whilst you are speaking to the family and be open about what you are writing and why. Make sure you ask how to pronounce names correctly, too.

Update information on your social work recording system as soon as possible. Make sure you review the information regularly. Household members may change, and people move addresses and change their telephone numbers regularly. Remember other professionals may rely on the information you obtain and record, such as a colleague or team manager in your absence, or an Independent Reviewing Officer (IRO) or Child Protection Conference Chair. Inaccurate or out-of-date information is at best irritating, and at worst dangerous.

Information can be recorded from historical case files and taken at face value, without source checking and verification. There are some instances where historical information is completely wrong, or repeated over a number of years, it can be misinterpreted and then reinterpreted like some kind of whispering game. Families may have a different recollection of events which happened historically, and this is absolutely fine. We will all recall past events in our own lives slightly differently to others who were involved. We all have our own narratives. When collating information from historical case files, ensure facts are obtained where possible, and any areas of ambiguity are recognised and acknowledged. Be clear of the source of the piece of information. Was this the opinion of a professional at the time? Was it information the child themselves shared? Is the information from a written report? Try not to reinterpret or re-word the information. We know that language, services and ways of working do change overtime. If the language you read is not the language you would usually use, then quote directly, again making clear the source of the information.

Seek the family's views regarding any past events you wish to include in current assessment work. This is really useful in terms of transparency and explaining to a family why you wish to include past information. Obtaining their views before analysis in the family's assessment is helpful. The family member's narrative on their past can be incorporated into your assessment, and any discrepancies or disagreements clearly noted. Use the family's own words to avoid misinterpretation. Again, if they do not speak in the way you might usually write, quote their views directly or ask the family member to write their own piece, to take ownership of their information and use this directly in your assessment or report. Building the confidence of a child, young person or family member in owning their story and collaborating with them on case recording is really powerful and inclusive.

Where there are additional barriers for a child, young person or their family members, make sure they are offered the right support in order for you to obtain accurate information. The most obvious is perhaps the use of an interpreter where English is a second language. This can sometimes be problematic in itself if the family's first language is a specific dialect. Sometimes interpreters are scarce. Families may fear the use of an interpreter due to cultural barriers. Do your very best to ensure the right interpreter for the family is able to support you, and take your time obtaining the basic information, and repeating back to clarify.

Where there is a parent with a learning or mental health need, always consider an independent advocate. Your organisation may commission advocacy services for children and adults, or you may need to refer to a specific organisation. The advocate can support you to approach the person in the right way, ensure they have understood your questions and comments, and that you have understood their responses accurately. The advocate will help with building trust and hopefully give the person confidence to engage. For those with a communication difficulty, consider if there is someone who can help, such as a professional or family member, who could assist you. There may be parental peer support or parent-led advocacy service in your area, where those with lived experience can directly support a parent or carer (Research in Practice, 2021). Such models are gaining momentum in practice, so consider new approaches to enable engagement.

A child with disabilities may have a support worker or learning mentor who knows them really well, a parent may have an excellent relationship with the child's named health professional or school. All these considerations will help you plan effectively and will give you the very best chance to obtain good quality and accurate information from the start.

Write the 'right' amount

This can be very tricky and actually there is no 'right' amount as such, and no 'perfect' example of a piece of case recording. Deciding what to write is subjective to some degree. There is a delicate balance between writing far too much and writing far too little. What we mean by writing the 'right' amount is attempting to strike a middle ground, where the information recorded is detailed enough to be useful, fit for purpose and develops the child's story. Case recording requires professional judgement and reflection. Cumbersome and lengthy case records lose impact, analysis, and lack focus. As we have already explored, this is not helpful to enabling families understand risks and strengths in their lives. Case recording which is minimal and sparse often lacks coherence and clarity, and essential information may be missed.

What can we do?

The first task, before we even start to write, is to consider the purpose of the recording. Who is the primary audience? What will this recording add to the child's story? How will this information be used in the future? This will impact on the way the case recording is structured, and how it is written, and ultimately how much we need to write.

For some shorter interactions, such as phone calls to and from professionals or to undertake a specific task with a family, it may be appropriate to record factual information, perhaps in the form of bullet points, making sure the key basic information is present. The date and time, full name, profession (if applicable) and contact details of the person involved, as well as the content of what happened. Other interactions may require more of a descriptive narrative to set the scene and describe something you have seen or heard, which is pertinent to the child's life. We always aim to be child-centred; this is the child's case file after all. We want to capture the child's views and the views of significant adults around them.

For more complex interactions such as longer home visits and meetings, it is really useful to make some basic notes first. This helps you to consider the key points you want to include and to structure the piece. This aids reflection and helps consider what aspects of the interaction are most important to include and why. Making a few basic notes will actually make writing the case record much easier, and less time consuming, as you'll have had opportunity to structure and plan. Often this stage is missed as social workers feel there is duplication, but without this step, writing longer pieces then becomes muddled and disjointed. Consider what the family would like to see recorded too and imagine them reading your case record whilst you write. This will help with the language you use and how the recording will flow.

Don't forget to differentiate between fact and opinion. Professional opinion is great, when clear and evidence-based. You could write a separate paragraph at the end of a recording, or if there are professional opinions throughout the recording, make sure you clearly state this is what it is.

 Ensure information shared is information understood

Social work frequently involves sharing and communicating information, but this is not a neutral action. As Calder asserts: information *"encompasses feelings, attitudes, beliefs, intentions and desires"* (Calder, 2016: 73). We need to be consciously aware of what we say, how we say it, and what exactly we mean when sharing written communication such as assessments, case records, letters and emails. It is often assumed that when information has been shared, it has been understood by the recipient and this is not always the case, as highlighted in many Safeguarding Children Practice Reviews and Serious Case Reviews.

What can we do?

Check, check, check! It sounds obvious right? But how often do we send a piece of written information, from an email to a completed assessment, and don't always check it has been received for shared understanding with the child, their family or other professionals? Use plain and simple language, avoiding acronyms and social work jargon. Checking information thoroughly on receipt from others is also helpful to ensure you have understood correctly, too, and that this information is recorded accurately. Finally, checking what you have written and how this is worded is essential, to make sure it has the right focus and tone for the child, young person or family member.

Getting into the habit of checking information with others on a regular basis is really helpful. You could follow up significant information you have sent with a brief phone call to ensure it has been received by the right family member or professional and have a short discussion about the content to clarify their understanding. Use open and exploratory questions and ask the recipient to share what they have understood from the written information, in their own words. This is especially important when circumstances change within the family or new decisions or plans have been made. When receiving information from others, ask if you don't understand what something means, rather than making assumptions. There is no shame in seeking to clarify information and saying, 'I don't understand'.

In relation to completing more in-depth assessments, it is good practice to provide the previous session written up for the family at the start of their next session. The family can see exactly what has been written and you can have an open discussion about any factual inaccuracies or misinterpretations. It is a chance to record the family's views along the way, and then the final assessment document should yield no surprises. This will also help you keep on top of case recording as you go. Views and opinions are gathered regularly, hopefully leading to an open working relationship with families, where trust is built.

 Dedicate time to case recording

Undoubtedly, this is one of the biggest challenges facing social workers, but the importance and complexity of case recording cannot be overlooked. Case recording is often seen as a separate and distinct entity to 'doing' social work, rather than a necessary and complementary part of social work as a whole. Without dedicating time to case recording, there may be a time delay between the event happening and the recording being completed which will impact on quality and accuracy. Rushed case notes may blur fact and opinion, and not provide the necessary space for reflection and analysis. Dedicating time to case recording ensures records remain up to date, that you respond to changes in circumstances, and that you value the usefulness of case recording in your practice.

What can we do?

Setting time aside in our diaries and sticking to this, is really helpful. However, we know, in reality this can be a huge challenge. It is tempting to slot other activities into this dedicated time when issues arise, and obviously as already acknowledged, there may be emergencies within your work which need an immediate response. For some social workers, completing case recording every day for a short period, say 30-45 minutes, at the very start or the very end of the day works really well. For others, it may be pencilling out a couple of hours at a time. Try and find somewhere quiet with minimal distractions so you can concentrate. Like many aspects of social work, it is finding a method that works for you. Some people can work well in a busy office, whilst others need a quiet space. Some people will concentrate better early morning and others into the evening. We are all different and that is fine. Keeping information up-to-date is key. Case recording little and often is more manageable than being overwhelmed by hours of recording a backlog. This is when mistakes can happen, and information is missed.

Timescales can be set for us, such as assessment deadlines or court reports. However, setting your own deadlines, a little earlier than the scheduled ones, can be really helpful (Dyke, 2019). This avoids a rush towards the due date and allows additional information to be added in as needed. Some deadlines set for us can encourage spending longer on the task than necessary and contribute to delay. Dyke shares, in his experience, *"social workers taking the longest to do their work, are not the ones producing the highest quality work"*, adding *"the only timescale that matters in practice is 'how quickly does the child / adult need me to do this?"* (Dyke, 2019: 165). If a child and family's needs can be assessed and all recording completed in a shorter period, then this will benefit the child and family, and you as a worker. Use your professional judgement, as putting off a task can also impact negatively on your mental health, with the task losing momentum (Dyke, 2019).

Consider having separate 'notebooks' for different activities. A small notebook or daily electronic log on your laptop could be used for notes regarding day-to-day activities such as phone calls, emails and other less complex day-to-day tasks which need to be recorded. This would allow you to make some basic notes before transferring information over to the social work system, hopefully making this task less cumbersome and more time efficient. Some very short activities may be recorded straight away, if you have the time. You could use a separate 'notebook', again paper or electronic, for more complex activities such as assessment sessions, observations of family time, and for recording meetings. Some social workers use a system where they keep all written notes for one particular family in one place, making it easy to refer back for information when larger reports and assessments are required. Also making it easier to find and record on the social work system at a later date. Ask your colleagues how they collate and organise information for children and families in their work. There will be a whole range of methods and ideas for you to try!

Be child-centred

Child-centred practice means giving priority to the child, promoting their right to participate in decisions affecting their lives, listening to children and building relationships with them: *"it is about seeing the world through their eyes, understanding what their day to day lived experience is really like"* (Race and O'Keefe, 2017: 4). A major criticism within Serious Case Reviews is often the child's voice being absent. In Laming's report (2003) into the tragic death of Victoria Climbie, he found Victoria's wishes and feelings were almost entirely missing from her own case file. Being child-centred does not mean ignoring context. The child's family, friends and wider community are all hugely important. It means locating the child's voice within this context: making sure the child is very much at the centre and their voice is heard in case recording. It also reflects the relationship you have with the child, such as shared hopes, aspirations and goals. How important are those to a child looking back on their records?

What can we do?

Make sure the excellent direct work with children that happens in social work every day is reflected in the child's file. This does not necessarily need to be reams and reams of typing. Get creative by taking photographs of the work you've completed with the child, such as pictures, drawings or games you've played. Use the words the child themselves has written in direct work. Consider the use of video or audio recordings of the child's voice if you're able and have necessary consents. Multi-task by asking the child to help review their child in need, child protection plan, or child looked after plan with you and write these documents alongside them on visits.

Frame the risks, strengths and needs in the child's life in relation to the impact on the child. Rather than write about adult issues, consider in your case recording how these adult issues impact on the child's day-to-day life. So, what is the impact of domestic abuse, substance misuse, or adult mental health issues on the child now? What is your evidence? What is the child saying, or for younger children, or those with additional needs, how are they responding, on observation, to these events? Be mindful that the same family issue may have a very different impact on each child within the family, depending on their age, development and level of understanding, and also, they have different relationships with the adults around them. By focussing on the impact on the individual children, it also makes analysis richer and increases our understanding and empathy of the child's experiences.

Ensure accessible, clear and appropriate language is used so the child, of sufficient age and understanding, can read recordings, reports and plans themselves. Where children are younger or have communication needs, consider writing a child friendly version of a report or plan that they can access and respond to. This may be in very simple language, be purely pictorial or even auditory if this suits the needs of the child. Think about the words you use. This has been a theme throughout the book, but valuable to keep reflecting upon. Any language used which blames a child for the abuse or neglect they experience, can compound trauma, so for example 'attention seeking behaviour' could be reframed as 'care seeking behaviour'. This is more compassionate, empathetic and positive to read for the child.

 Work as a team

Case recording is often regarded as an individual task or sole responsibility, and this is to some extent very accurate. A child usually has one primary social worker allocated to their case, and this person is responsible for case recording on the child's case file. However, when we consider the complexities of case recording, the time this takes, and significance of getting this right for the child and family, there are many ways social workers can support each other in case recording.

What can we do?

If you are struggling with case recording and are feeling anxious or worried in managing your time, do ask for support at an early stage. This could involve an informal discussion with your team manager, or be part of more formal supervision. Think about what aspect of case recording you are finding challenging and seek advice and support. There may be a colleague within your team that could help you reflect and consider practical ways to make case recording work for you or consider 'good practice in case recording' as a regular topic within your team meeting, when workers can share tips and things they have found useful. As we have shared, managing case recording is often a challenge for social workers, so you certainly won't be alone.

A practical tip for managing longer assessment sessions is to co-work with a colleague. One social worker would plan and lead the session with the child or family member, and the second social worker would be responsible for recording contemporaneous notes and updating the social work system. You can take this in turns for each session. Co-working allows for a more open and relaxed conversation between the lead social worker and the family member and can enhance relationship building. This method helps with reflection on the case, especially for complex assessments, as having a second person involved aids analysis. You can consider the child's situation from different perspectives. You will undoubtedly learn from each other and be able to provide constructive feedback, which is also incredibly valuable. Notes will be more accurate taken by a secondary worker, who can concentrate on this task alone. It is really helpful to write the question posed by the lead social worker as well as the response from the family member, as accurately as possible, so you have the context when reflecting back and analysing the information. This also ensures information has not been misinterpreted or reinterpreted when notes are not taken comprehensively.

Student social workers regularly read case records, chronologies, assessments and reports as part of their placement, and are asked to learn from others around them. On qualification this, on the whole, becomes less commonplace. It can be a missed opportunity for ongoing learning from peers. Consider buddying up with a colleague to provide constructive feedback on each other's work; lead an exercise in your team meeting to explore case recording as a tool to analyse; ask your team manager for individualised advice and guidance on how your writing could be improved and what you are doing well. Consider creative ways to case record that your team could perhaps trial, with the support from your service managers. Have proactive conversations about what would make case recording more streamlined and family focused. Share good practice and celebrate the excellent work you are doing every day!

Conclusion

This final chapter has drawn together learning from the whole guide to concentrate on practical tips which will help you establish good case recording every day. We have shared creative tips and ideas for you to try in your own case recording, as well as within teams, sharing your knowledge and skills with others. Some small changes to daily practice can create huge differences to how case recording is viewed and completed. Case recording well will guide your social work practice, helping you make more analytical decisions alongside children and families. In conclusion, we would like you to consider the following questions:

What are you going to do now in your own social work practice?

Why are these things your focus?

How will you make sure you commit to good quality case recording?

 ## Talking it Through

It is always important to extend your learning and talking things through with others can be helpful. At the end of each chapter we include a link to a video showing some students and / or practitioners talking through the content and their learning. In this final video Siobhan and Rebecca meet with Brett again. Brett is a social work student, and he previously joined us to discuss chapter 1. We are also joined by Sarah, a social work student, and Elly an experienced social worker working in a young offenders institute. The discussion not only explores learning from this chapter but also suggests ways in which the book could be used by practice educators and in CPD groups.

Epilogue

The Future of Case Recording

We want to acknowledge that this book has been written against the backdrop of the Covid-19 pandemic, which has had a profound impact on how we respond and practice as social workers. The pandemic has forced us to think differently and respond with new and innovative ways of working, including in relation to case recording.

Social workers have engaged with families by video call and socially distanced meet ups, held virtual meetings with multi-agency colleagues, undertaken assessment sessions by telephone and video link, and supported family time for those children and young people away from their families in a virtual world. Text, email and social media; we have used technology like never before. This range of media presents the opportunity to use material to record *"the child's world, in the child's voice, on their file for their future reference"* (Everard, 2020). It is not to say all of these approaches have always been the very best we can offer families, and some methods of engagement have been a necessity through an unprecedented crisis, rather than what we would ideally choose for those with whom we work with. However, as with all new approaches, our skills have been sharpened and our minds have focused on the strengths and new possibilities we can take forward to the post Covid world. Put succinctly by Zywek et al. (2020):

"The chaos imposed upon our current ordered systems arguably represents a dramatic shift from opposite polarities: the uncertainty caused by Covid-19 provides us with, at the very least, an opportunity to consider new ways of understanding. We have witnessed changes on a systemic level that previously appeared unfeasible; this provides an extraordinary window of unimagined possibilities."

How does this impact on case recording?

The changes brought about by Covid-19 and services responses have certainly made us consider how we can use and promote the use of technology to support case recording. It has been highlighted many times that case recording and processes take up a huge chunk of a social workers' precious time, taking them away from face-to-face interactions with families. We have shared our view that case recording is an essential part of social work, which can help build and maintain relationships with those we work with. However, we would also advocate for streamlining processes which support the social worker in keeping case recording relevant and up-to-date, and increase collaboration with the child, young person or family. Technology can really help.

Anecdotally, in our practice experience, some families have shared they feel more comfortable engaging in meetings virtually from their own home, rather than sitting in a room with professionals. They have told us that they feel less intimidated and nervous in online child protection conferences, child in need meetings and core group meetings, for example. Extended relatives have joined such meetings from different parts of the country, and even from abroad. Children and young people have participated in their meetings from other venues, such as school, minimising disruption to their day and helping them access support from adults in a safe space. There are definite complexities to holding virtual meetings, and we do not propose they are always the best approach for all families. Yet virtual meetings continue and can be positive in supporting the needs of children, young people and families. Sometimes they are the best option.

In relation to case recording, technology has presented us with the possibility to video or audio record formal meetings, which could actually form the basis of the case record. Do we then need a written record typing at all, or perhaps just a summary document? Could audio and video recordings of virtual meetings be uploaded onto the social work system, and be viewed later? These questions are not so straightforward. There needs to be careful consideration of a range of issues including the informed consent of children, families and professionals who participate, in addition to adherence to data protection legislation, and measured thought about how and with whom the video or audio recording can be shared. However, this does present us with real possibilities for the future, to make the task of case recording more efficient for social workers, and the child's case record more visual and accessible than ever before.

Everard (2020) highlights a further example: the recording of family time. Family time for children and young people who are care experienced has, at times, had to take place virtually by video or phone calls, due to Covid-19 restrictions. This has the capacity to video or audio record, providing the potential opportunity for children to view or hear their family time in the future. This would be a powerful way for children to see and hear their interactions with loved ones, years ahead. Everard also feels the key to empowerment is helping children and families choose how they want to interact with their case records, stating:

"Do they want to read them, or comment on them or are they in a position to assist writing them? Would they prefer this to be done via phone calls, emails, letters, texts or in another format? Some young people may engage with being recorded and have this placed on their file for the future, and others may not. I think the key here is that we have a number of different approaches and we work with people to record their stories in the best way for them."

(Everard, 2020)

Children, young people and families participating in case recording, may possibly reduce anxiety for families, balance the power, and help families truly engage in decisions affecting their lives. The Transparency Project (2018) considered why parents may want to record meetings themselves with social workers and other professionals, such as on a mobile phone. They found, amongst other things, that parents don't want to forget information and don't want to rely on the accounts of others. Some families actually do case record themselves now, so how can we support and collaborate with them, rather than dismiss or vilify this practice? There are already technologies available to support such work. Schools and nurseries, for example, sometimes use electronic platforms which are password protected with staff and parents sharing information, stories and photographs of the child's experiences, learning and development (Everard, 2020). Why not for social work?

Social work continues to advance and adapt in our ever-changing world, and we look forward to seeing how practice progresses, and case recording evolves, to support the needs of children, young people and families in the future. We hope this guide has sparked reflection and fuelled creativity to create opportunities for high quality case recording when working with children and families.

The 10 Principles

 Privilege

Social workers are in a position of great privilege. We often come into the lives of children and their families when they are at their most vulnerable. When we see case recording as the privilege that it is, we will do it better.

Why *is case recording so important?*

 Permanence

Case recording is the most permanent form of communication. Many years from now an adult might be reading what you are writing about them as a child now.

What *do I want the child or young person to see?*

 Priority

It is important to prioritise case recording. It is often the last thing on a social worker's list. Perhaps we need to rethink this. Case recording should never be seen as a chore. It is a core part of the role and enhances other areas of practice, such as reflection, analysis and decision making.

How *do I prioritise case recording?*

 Purpose

It is important to be clear about the purpose of our work in social work. Always think about the purpose and audience of any case recording.

Why *am I writing this case record and who is it for?*

 Partnership

It is important to take a partnership approach to case recording and promote participation of children, young people and family members. Working with them and involving them in our case recording processes wherever possible.

How *can I work in partnership with children and families?*

Positivity

Social workers need to be strengths-based and highlight the positives in the lives of children, young people and families. These positives need to be evident in case records. This does not mean ignoring risk and needs but making sure case recording is balanced.

What *can I record which is positive and strengths based?*

 Power

Social workers are in a position of power. We have access to lots of personal and sensitive information. We decide what information is important to record. We choose the words to write and the language we use.

How *do I reduce the power differential?*

 Presentation

How you write is important. We have highlighted that information needs to be presented in a clear way, which is accessible and well written. The small details, such as the spelling of names and places, really matter.

How *can I present case recording well?*

 Planning

Reflecting for action, planning ahead, is vital in social work for a whole range of reasons. We have demonstrated how planning ahead helps good record keeping. Case recording also influences reflection on action. Plans for children and young people need to be based on reflection, analysis and comprehensive decision-making.

How *can I plan effectively to support good case recording?* **How** *do I make sure case recording supports good planning?*

 Policy

Your own employer will have policies which relate to case recording. Make sure that you are familiar with the policies that you need to work within.

What *do I need to know from my own organisation?*

References

ADCS (2015) *The role of serious case reviews in improving the child protection system.* (Manchester) ADCS.

Baginsky, M., Moriarty, J., Manthorpe, J., Stevens, M., MacInnes, T., and Nagendran, T. (2010) *Social Workers workload survey: Messages from the frontline.* (London) Department for Children, Schools and Families.

Bedford, A. (2015) *Serious Case Review into Child Sexual Exploitation in Oxfordshire: from the experiences of Children A, B, C, D, E, and F.* (Oxford) Oxford Safeguarding Children Board.

Bernard, C. and Harris, P. (2016) *Safeguarding Black Children: Good Practice in Child Protection.* (London) Jessica Kingsley.

Borton, T. (1970) *Reach, Teach and Touch.* (London) McGraw Hill.

Bradford Safeguarding Children's Board (BSCB) (2013) *A Serious Case Review: Hamza Khan. An overview report.* (Bradford) Bradford Safeguarding Children's Board.

Brandon, M., Belderson, P., Warren, C., Howe, D., Gardner, R., Dodsworth, J., Black, J. (2008) *Analysing child deaths and serious injury through abuse and neglect: What can we learn? A biennial analysis of Serious Case Reviews 2003–2005.* (Nottingham) Department of Children, Schools and Families.

Brandon, M., Sidebotham, P., Belderson, P., Cleaver, H., Dickens, J., Garstang, J., Harris, J., Sorensen, J. and Wate, R. (2020) *Complexity and challenge: a triennial analysis of SCRs 2014-2017.* (London) Department for Education.

Brown, S., Brady, G., Franklin, A. and Crookes, R. (2017) *The use of tools and checklists to assess risk of child sexual exploitation: An exploratory study.* (Coventry) Coventry University. Available online at: https://www.csacentre.org.uk/our-research/responding-to-csa/risk-tools/ Accessed on 27/12/2022.

BASW. (2018) *Professional Capabilities Framework: Social worker.* (London) BASW.

BASW. (2021) Code of Ethics. (Birmingham) BASW Available online at; https://www.basw.co.uk/system/files/resources/basw_code_of_ethics_-_2021.pdf Accessed on 30/08/2022.

Brown, L., Moore, S. and Turney, D. (2012) Analysis and Critical Thinking in Assessment. Resource Pack – Core Publication. (Dartington) Research in Practice.

Calder, M. (2016) *Risk in Child Protection: Assessment challenges and frameworks for practice.* (London) Jessica Kingsley.

Care Inspectorate. (2017) *Practice Guide to Chronologies.* Dundee: Care Inspectorate. Available online at: www.careinspectorate.com/images/ documents/3670/Practice%20guide%20to%20chronologies%202017.pdf Accessed on 23/08/2022.

Carter, M. and Maclean, S. (2022) *Insiders Outsiders: Hidden Narratives of Care Experienced Social Workers.* (Lichfield) Kirwin Maclean Associates.

Carvalho, S. and White, H. (1997). Combining the quantitative and qualitative approaches to poverty measurement and analysis: The practice and the potential. World Bank Technical Paper 366. (Washington, D.C.) World Bank.

Child Safeguarding Practice Review Panel. (2020) *Annual Report 2018 to 2019: Patterns in practice, key messages, and 2020 work programme.* (London) The Safeguarding Practice Panel.

Child Safeguarding Practice Review Panel. (2022) *Child Protection in England: National review into the murders of Arthur Labinjo-Hughes and Star Hobson.* (London) The Safeguarding Practice Panel.

The Children's Society. (2021) *Defining Criminal Exploitation.* Available online at https://www.childrenssociety.org.uk/information/professionals/resources/ defining-child-criminal-exploitation Accessed 27/12/2022.

Coram Voice. (2015) *Children and Young People's Views on Being in Care A Literature Review.* Bristol: University of Bristol and Coram Voice. Available online: https://coramvoice.org.uk/wp-content/uploads/2021/01/Childrens-views-lit-review-FINAL-2.pdf Accessed on 6/5/2022.

Dalzell, R. and Sawyer, E. (2011) *Putting Analysis into Assessment: Undertaking Assessments of Need. A Toolkit for Practitioners* (2nd edition). (London) National Children's Bureau.

Department for Education. (2010) *IRO Handbook: Statutory guidance for independent reviewing officers and local authorities on their functions in relation to case management and review for looked after children.* (Nottingham) DCSF publications.

Department for Education. (2015) *The Children Act 1989 guidance and regulations Volume 2: care planning, placement and case review.* (London) Department of Education.

Department for Education. (2017) *Child sexual exploitation. Definition and a guide for practitioners, local leaders and decision makers working to protect children from child sexual exploitation.* (London) Department for Education.

Department of Education. (2018) *Applying corporate parenting principles to looked-after children and care leavers. Statutory guidance for local authorities.* (London) Department of Education.

Department for Education. (2019) *Child Safeguarding Practice Review Panel: practice guidance.* (London) Department of Education.

Department for Education. (2021) *Press release: Government action following murder of Arthur Labinjo-Hughes.* Published 5th December 2021. HM Government. Available online at: https://www.gov.uk/government/news/government-action-following-murder-of-arthur-labinjo-hughes Accessed 20/9/2022

Department for Education. (2022) *Press release: Bradford children's services to be placed into Trust.* Published 25th January 2022. (London) HM Government. Available online at: https://www.gov.uk/government/news/bradford-childrens-services-to-be-placed-into-trust Accessed on 6/02/2022.

Donovan, T. (2016) *Social worker struck off after disclosing case details.* Community care online. Available from: http://www.communitycare.co.uk/2016/04/27/social-worker-struck-disclosingdetails-families-using-personal-laptop/ Accessed on 27/12/2022.

Driscol, J. (2000) Practising Clinical Supervision. (London) Balliere Tindall.

Dyke, C. (2019) *Writing Analytical Assessments in Social Work* (2nd edn) (St Albans) Critical Publishing.

Eaton, J. and Holmes, D. (2017) *Working Effectively to Address Child Sexual Exploitation: Evidence Scope.* (Devon) Research in Practice.

Elsley, S. (2010) *Media Coverage of Child Deaths in the UK: The Impact of baby P: A Case for Influence? CLiCP Briefing.* (Edinburgh) The University of Edinburgh/NSPCC.

Everard, K. (2020) 'Can children and young people ever 'own' their record?' in *Social Work 2020-21 under Covid-19 Magazine. 4th Edition, published 2nd June 2020.* Available online at: https://sites.google.com/sheffield.ac.uk/sw2020-21-covid19/editions/4th-edition-2-june-2020/can-children-young-people-and-their-families-own-their-records Accessed on 29/08/2022

Featherstone, B., Gupta, A., Morris, K. and White, S. (2018) *Protecting Children: A social model.* (London) Policy Press.

Ferguson, H. (2016) 'Making home visits: Creativity and the embodied practices of home visiting in social work and child protection'. *Qualitative Social Work*, 17 (1), pp. 65–80.

Firmin, C., Horan, J., Holmes, D. and Hopper, D. (2019). *Safeguarding during adolescence – the relationship between Contextual Safeguarding, Complex Safeguarding and Transitional Safeguarding.* (Devon) Research in Practice.

Firmin, C. (2020) *Contextual Safeguarding and Child Protection: Rewriting the rules.* (London) Taylor and Francis.

Fook, J., Ryan, M. and Hawkins, L. (2000) Professional Expertise: Practice, theory and education for working in uncertainty. (London) Whiting and Birch.

Goldsmith, L. (1999) Recording with Care: Inspection of Case Recording in Social Services Departments. (London) Social Services Inspectorate and Department of Health.

Gov.uk (2021) Statistics and data: Children Looked after in England including adoptions. Available online at https://explore-education-statistics.service.gov.uk/find-statistics/children-looked-after-in-england-including-adoptions/2021 Accessed on 29/08/2022.

The Guardian. (2001) *Timeline for the Climbie Case*. Published 24th September 2001. Available online at.: www.theguardian.com/society/2001/sep/24/childrensservices Accessed on 29/08/2022.

The Guardian. (2010) *The tragedy of Khyra Ishaq's death*. Published 25th February 2010. Available online at: https://www.theguardian.com/uk/2010/feb/25/khyra-ishaq-starving-death-background Accessed on 06/02/2022.

Haringey Local Safeguarding Children's Board. (2008) *Serious Case Review: Child A*. (London) Haringey LSCB.

Healy, K. and Mulholland, J. (2019) *Writing Skills for Social Workers* (3rd edn). (London) Sage.

Hartman, A. (1995) 'Diagrammatic Assessment of Family Relationships.' *Families in Society*. 76 (2), pp. 111-112.

Heyes, S. and Fen Hui, C. (2015). *The adolescent brain: vulnerability and opportunity*. UNICEF. Available online at: https://www.unicef-irc.org/article/1149-the-adolescent-brain-vulnerability-and-opportunity.html Accessed on 30/3/2022.

Hicks, L. and Stein, M. (2015) 'Understanding and working with adolescent neglect: perspectives from research, young people and professionals'. *Child and Family Social Work*. 20 (2), pp. 223-233.

HM Government. (2018) *Working Together to Safeguard Children: A guide to inter-agency working to safeguard and promote the welfare of children*. (London) Department for Education.

Holmes, L. and McDermid, S. (2013) 'How social workers spend their time in frontline children's social care in England'. *Journal of Childrens Services*. 8 (2), pp.123 - 133.

Home Office. (2018) *Criminal Exploitation of children and vulnerable adults: County Lines guidance*. (London) Home Office.

Hood, R. (2018) *Complexity in Social Work*. (London) Sage.

Hoyle, V., Shepherd, E., Flinn, A. and Lomas, E. (2019) 'Child Social-Care Recording and the Information Rights of Care-Experienced People: A Recordkeeping Perspective'. British Journal of Social Work. 49 (7), pp. 1856–1874.

Information Commissioner's Office. (2021) Guide to the General Data Protection Regulation (GDPR). Available online at: https://ico.org.uk/media/for-organisations/guide-to-data-protection/guide-to-the-general-data-protection-regulation-gdpr-1-1.pdf Accessed on 30/08/2022.

Independent Care Review Scotland. (2020) *The Promise.* Available online at =: https://www.carereview.scot/wp-content/uploads/2020/02/The-Promise.pdf Accessed on 29/08/2022.

Jay, A. (2014) *Independent Inquiry into Child Sexual Exploitation in Rotherham.* (Rotherham) Metropolitan Borough Council.

Jones, P. (2009). *Second Serious Case Review Overview Report relating to Peter Connelly.* (London) Haringey LSCB.

Jones, R. (2016) 'Writing skills for social workers' in Davies, K. and Jones, R. (Eds) *Skills for Social Work Practice.* (London) Palgrave.

Killion, J., & Todnem, G. (1991). A process for personal theory building. *Educational Leadership, 48(7),* 14-16.

Klonowski, A. (2013) *Report of the Independent Reviewing Officer in Relation to Child Sexual Exploitation Issues in Rochdale Metropolitan Borough Council During the Period 2006 to 2013.* (Rochdale) Rochdale Metropolitan Borough Council.

Laming, Lord. (2003) *The Victoria Climbie Inquiry.* (London) The Stationery Office.

Leeds City Council. (2021) *One minute guide: restorative practice.* Available online at: https://www.leeds.gov.uk/docs/One%20minute%20guides/One%20Minute%20Guide%20-%20Restorative%20Practice.pdf Accessed on 29/08/2022.

Lillis, T., Leedham, M., and Twine, A. (2020) Time, the Written Record, and Professional Practice: The Case of Contemporary Social Work. *Written Communication.* 37 (4), pp. 431–486.

Lillis, T. and Vallely, J. (2021) Writing analysis in social care - What do we mean by analysis? (iriss.org.uk) Available online. Accessed 24.12.2022

Lock, R. (2013) *Serious Case Review: Re Daniel Pelka Born 15th July 2007 Died 3rd March 2012.* (Coventry) Coventry Safeguarding Children Board.

MacAlister, J. (2022) *The independent review of children's social care: Final report.* (London) The Independent Review of Children's Social Care.

Maclean, S. (2019) *Working Towards Accreditation Putting the Pieces Together. A Workbook for Child and Family Social Workers.* (Lichfield) Kirwin Maclean Associates.

Maclean, S. and Harrison, R. (2015) *Theory and Practice: A Straightforward Guide for Social Work Students.* (Lichfield) Kirwin Maclean Associates.

McCormack, P. Y. (2022) *Marks of an Unwanted Rainbow.* (Lichfield) Kirwin Maclean Associates.

McIntyre, N. and Pegg, D. (2018) Councils use 377,000 people's data in efforts to predict child abuse. The Guardian online. https://www.theguardian.com/society/2018/sep/16/councils-use-377000-peoplesdata-in-efforts-to-predict-child-abuse Accessed 28.12.2022

Ministry of Justice. (2021) *Practice direction 12a - care, supervision and other part 4 proceedings: guide to case management.* Available online at: https://www.justice.gov.uk/courts/procedure-rules/family/practice_directions/pd_part_12a Accessed on 23/8/2022.

Moray Council. (No date) *Preparing for Multi-Agency Meetings.* Available online at http://www.moray.gov.uk/moray_standard/page_79759.html Accessed on 29/08/2022.

Munro, E. (2002) *Effective Child Protection.* (London) Sage.

Munro, E. (2011) *The Munro review of child protection-final report: a child centred system.* (London) The Stationery Office.

Mullan, R. (2014) *Training should produce social workers well-acquainted with the sector.* In Guardian online. Available online at: https://www.theguardian.com/social-care-network/2014/feb/18/martin-neary-social-workers-education Accessed 27/12/2022

NSPCC. (2021) *Statistics briefing: child deaths due to abuse or neglect.* (London) NSPCC.

National Statistics. (2021) *Characteristics of children in need. Published 28th October 2021.* (London) HM Government. Available online at: https://explore-education-statistics.service.gov.uk/find-statistics/characteristics-of-children-in-need/2021#releaseHeadlines-summary Accessed on 06/02/2022

Nicolas, J. (2015) 'Why do home visits matter in child protection?' *Community care.* Available online at: https://www.communitycare.co.uk/2015/09/02/home-visits-matter-child-protection/ Accessed on 29/8/2022.

Ofsted. (2014) *In the child's time: professional responses to neglect.* Available online at: https://assets.publishing.service.gov.uk/government/uploads/system/uploads/attachment_data/file/419072/In_the_child_s_time-professional_responses_to_neglect.pdf Accessed on 27/12/2022.

Parker, S. (2017) *Social Work Practice: Assessment, Planning, Intervention and Review.* (London) Sage.

Pemberton, C. (2010) 'Danger signs that lay in a timeline. How social workers should use case chronologies.' *Community Care.* Available online at: https://www.communitycare.co.uk/2010/09/27/danger-signs-that-lay-in-a-timeline-how-social-workers-should-use-case-chronologies/ Accessed on 26/08/2022.

Pritchard, J. and Leslie, S. (2011) *Recording Skills in Safeguarding Adults: Best Practice and Evidential Requirements.* (London) Jessica Kingsley.

Race, T. and O'Keefe, R. (2017) *Child-Centred Practice: A handbook for social work.* (London) Palgrave.

Radford, J. (2010) *Serious Case Review Under Chapter VIII 'Working Together to Safeguard Children' In respect of the Death of a Child Case Number 14.* (Birmingham) Birmingham Children's Safeguarding Board.

Rai, L. (2014) *Effective writing for social work: making a difference.* (Bristol) Policy Press.

Raws, P. (2016) *Understanding Adolescent Neglect: Troubled Teens A study of the links between parenting and adolescent neglect.* (London) The Children's Society.

Research in Practice (2014) *Key messages: Developing and monitoring effective care plans.* Available online at: https://fosteringandadoption.rip.org.uk/wp-content/uploads/2014/05/DfE-12-Developing-and-Monitoring-Effective-Care-Plans-Final-PDF.pdf Accessed on 29/08/2022.

Rogers, M. (2020) *Writing Skills for Practice.* In Rogers, M., Whitaker, D., Edmondson, D. and Peach, D. Developing Skills and Knowledge for Social Work Practice. (London) Sage.

Rogers, M. and Allen, D. (2019) *Applying Critical Thinking and Analysis in Social Work.* (London) Sage.

Rolfe, G., Freshwater, D. and Jasper, M. (2001) Critical Reflection in Nursing and the Helping Professions: A User's Guide. (Basingstoke) Palgrave Macmillan.

Sissay, L. (2020) *My Name is Why?* (Edinburgh) Canongate books.

SCIE (2016) *Learning into Practice: Inter-professional communication and decision making – practice issues identified in 38 serious case reviews.* Available online at: Practice issues from serious case reviews – learning into practice – SCIE Accessed on 22/8/2022.

Safeguarding Survivor (2018) 'Divisive, demeaning and devoid of feeling: how social work jargon causes problems for families'. *Community Care.* Available online at : https://www.communitycare.co.uk/2018/05/10/divisive-demeaning-devoid-feeling-social-work-jargon-causes-problems-families/ Accessed on 29/08/2022.

Schön, D. (1983) *The Reflective Practitioner.* (London) Temple Smith.

Shannon, B. (2019) *Rewriting Social Care-Words that make me go mmmm.* Available online at: https://rewritingsocialcare.blog/2019/08/09/why-language-matters Accessed on 22/8/2022.

Sinek, S. (2019) *Start with Why: How Great Leaders Inspire Everyone to Take Action.* (London) Penguin Business.

Sinek, S. with Mead, D. and Docker, P. (2017) *Find Your Why: A Practical Guide For Discovering Purpose For You And Your Team.* (London) Penguin Random House.

Social Work Action Group. (2021) *Language in Social Work video.* Accessed on 29/08/2022 at https://www.youtube.com/watch?v=70k6MkxuZRU

Social Work England. (2019) *Professional Standards.* Available online at: https://www.socialworkengland.org.uk/standards/professional-standards/ Accessed on 29/08/2022.

Social Work Toolbox. (2019) *Eco-map activity.* Available online at: www.socialworkerstoolbox.com/ecomap-activity/ Accessed on 23/08/2022.

Stanley, Y. (2019) *What makes an effective case record?* Available online at: https://socialcareinspection.blog.gov.uk/2019/07/24/what-makes-an-effective-case-record/ Accessed on 26/08/2022.

TACT. (2019) *Language that cares Changing the way professionals talk about Children in Care.* (London) TACT.

The Transparency Project. (2018) *Parents recording social workers: A guidance note for parents and professionals.* Available online at: http://www.transparencyproject.org.uk/wp-content/uploads/Whymightparentswanttorecordmeetingsv3mar18.pdf Accessed on 9/7/2021.

Trevithick, P. (2012) *Social Work Skills and Knowledge, (3rd edn): A Practice Handbook.* (Maidenhead) Open University Press.

Turnell, A. and Edwards, S. (1999). Signs of Safety: A safety and solution-oriented approach to child protection casework. (New York) WW Norton.

Turney, D. (2016) 'Child Neglect and Black Children' in Bernard, C and Harris, P (Eds). *Safeguarding Black Children: Good Practice in Child Protection.* (London) Jessica Kingsley.

Turney, D., Platt, D., Selwyn., J and Farmer., (2011) *Social work assessment of children in need: what do we know/ messages from research.* (London) DFE

What Works for Children's Social Care. (2019a) *Shared Decision-Making: What is good practice in delivering meetings? Involving families meaningfully in decision-making to keep children safely at home: A rapid realist review.* (Cardiff) University of Cardiff.

What Works for Children's Social Care. (2019b) *Supporting Shared Decision-Making Meetings: Delivery, Implementation and Evaluation.* Available online at https://whatworks-csc.org.uk/wp-content/uploads/WWCSC_Shared_Decision_Making_Practice_guide.pdf Accessed on 29/08/2022.

Who Cares? Scotland. (2019) *Our lives, our stories, our records: A record access campaign.* Available online at: WCS-Report-Care-Records-Access-Campaign-August-2019.pdf (whocaresscotland.org) Accessed on 29/08/2022.

Wilkins, D. (2016) Guide to developing social work care plans. *Community Care Inform.* Available online at: https://www.researchgate.net/publication/307864588_Guide_to_developing_social_work_care_plans Accessed on 29/08/2022.

Wilkins, D. and Boahen, G. (2013) Critical Analysis Skills for Social Workers. (Maidenhead) OU Press.

Wilkins, D., Lynch, A. and Antonopoulou, V. (2018) 'A golden thread? The relationship between supervision, practice, and family engagement in child and family social work'. *Child and Family Social Work.* 23 (3), pp. 494-503

Wrench, K. and Naylor, L. (2013) *Life Story Work for Children who are Fostered or Adopted: Creative ideas and activities.* (London) Jessica Kingsley.

Zywek, L., Davis, E. and Devine, R. (2020) 'Child Protection Practice in an evolving era'. *Social Work 2020-21 under Covid-19 Magazine. 2nd Edition, published 24th April 2020.* Available online at: https://sw2020covid19.group.shef. ac.uk/2020/04/24/child-protection-practice-in-an-evolving-era/ Accessed on 29/08/2022.